KU-079-251

Preface

In 1960 the University of Leeds gave me a Research Fellowship, for which I shall always be grateful. My task was to make a historical survey of the training of teachers in England and Wales in the twentieth century.

That necessarily involved looking at nineteenth century training. I quickly became convinced that the story must be told as a whole if twentieth century developments were to be seen in perspective.

It is a long and complicated story. The brief summary of it which I offer in these pages—an abridgment of a longer manuscript—contains only a bare outline. I hope nevertheless that students in training to be teachers, for whom it is especially intended, will find it of some interest.

I have been helped by far more people than I can mention here. I would like particularly to thank Lord Morris of Grasmere and Professor Roy Niblett, who secured my Fellowship; and, for giving me valuable information, Miss M A B Jones, Miss K Nahapiet, Miss O M Stanton, Mrs C Townshend (née Tomkin), Mr A H Body, Mr E L Bradby, Mr J W Bridgeman, Mr R Brooke, Sir Alexander and Lady Ewing, Mr D W Humphreys, the Rev H Trevor Hughes, Mr D Jordan, the Rev A Price, Mr J M Rawcliffe, Dr R W Rich, Dr Akhtar Shakoor (Ph D thesis), and Professor N R Tempest. I wish to thank also Mr Stanley Foster of Hodder and Stoughton and his colleagues for their invariably friendly and helpful assistance.

I alone am responsible for the contents of the book.

Whatlington, East Sussex.   *H C Dent*
July 1976

LIBRARY, ST. PATRICK'S COLLEGE, DUBLIN 9
LEABHARLANN, COLÁISTE PHÁDRAIG, B.Á.C. 9

000121707

The Training ~~of Teach~~ *Nales*

ST. PATRICK'S
COLLEGE

LIBRARY

WITHDRAWN

WITHDRAWN

WITHDRAWN

The Training of Teachers in England and Wales 1800–1975

H C Dent

ST. PATRICK'S
COLLEGE
LIBRARY

HODDER AND STOUGHTON

LONDON SYDNEY AUCKLAND TORONTO

√ 0361 8017

Leabharlann
Colaiste Phádraig

ACC. 121707
CLASS 370·7/DEN
DATE 16/8/95
PRICE
DROIM CONRACH

ISBN 0 340 19751 X Boards
ISBN 0 340 19750 1 Unibook

Copyright © 1977 H C Dent
All rights reserved. No part of this publication may be reproduced or
transmitted in any form or by any means, electronic or mechanical,
including photocopy, recording, or any information storage and
retrieval system, without permission in writing from the publisher.

Printed and bound in Great Britain for
Hodder and Stoughton Educational,
a division of Hodder and Stoughton Ltd,
Mill Road, Dunton Green, Sevenoaks, Kent,
at the Benham Press, by William Clowes & Sons Ltd,
Colchester, Beccles and London.

Contents

LIBRARY
ST. PATRICK'S
COLLEGE

CHAPTER ONE

Foundations

Systematic training of school teachers did not begin in Britain until the nineteenth century. But gestures towards it were made in the eighteenth, notably by the Society for Promoting Christian Knowledge (SPCK), founded by members of the Church of England in 1699 to combat "the growth of Vice and Debauchery, especially among the poorer sort".[1]

A principal means adopted by the SPCK was the provision of 'Charity' schools, designed to help parents "desirous of having their Children taught, but . not able to afford them a Christian and Useful Education".[2] In these schools children learned to read the Bible and memorise the Church of England Liturgy. They might also be taught handwriting, and the boys a little arithmetic, the girls plain needlework.

As the aim of the Charity schools was the salvation of souls rather than the nurture of minds, the SPCK did not look so much for scholarship in its teachers as for religious orthodoxy and moral probity. In brief, the Society wanted communicant members of the Anglican Church, twenty-five years old or more, "of Sober Life and Conversation" and "a Meek Temper and Humble Behaviour". Scholastically, it was satisfied if male applicants had "a good Genius (i.e. aptitude) for Teaching", could write "a good Hand", and understood "the Grounds of Arithmetic". Women were not ordinarily expected to teach arithmetic, but they were supposed to be "sufficiently grounded in the English tongue" to be able to teach reading, and to be proficient in sewing and knitting.[3]

Academically, not very ambitious. But at least the SPCK

demanded *some* qualifications, and thus showed itself ahead of its age, which saw nothing untoward in entrusting the education of children of poor people to the aged, the decrepit, and the dissolute. The early leaders of the Society also realised that school-teaching, if not a learned profession, was at any rate a skilled craft, and that therefore its practitioners ought to be trained. They considered establishing a 'Normal School' (i.e. training college), but unfortunately never commanded the necessary funds. So they abandoned that idea—but not the idea of training.

They evolved various means for assisting recruits to become competent teachers. They commissioned the Revd Dr James Talbot, vicar of Spofforth in Yorkshire, to write a manual of guidance. He produced *The Christian Schoolmaster;* published in 1707, it remained in use throughout the eighteenth century. They urged school managers to give newly joined teachers the opportunity to observe and practise with experienced ones, encouraged country teachers to come to the capital to study at first hand the 'London' method commended in *The Christian Schoolmaster,* and organised a scheme of secondment whereby " 'eminent London teachers' voluntarily exiled themselves in the country to teach their method in urban and village schools".[4]

Most interestingly, some schools adopted a form of apprenticeship which anticipated the nineteenth century monitorial and pupil-teacher schemes.

> Promising elder lads taught the children under the master's superintendence, and, if they showed genius for teaching, they were apprenticed so that they "might gain the art of teaching school on the old master's methods".[5]

Despite such initiatives, it is doubtful whether training was ever widespread. The historian of the SPCK, Mr W K Lowther Clarke, says bluntly that "There was no training except by visiting schools where the new methods were in use".[6] In general, he is doubtless right, though possibly occasional attempts at more intensive training were made in London or at one or other of the SPCK's four 'Model Schools' in the provinces.[7]

As the century proceeds, references to training become rare. But it is recorded of the Revd Griffith Jones, founder of the Welsh 'Circulating Schools' that not only did he choose his teachers with extreme care, but also that:

Before being let loose on their charges, they were brought together for training ... "for some weeks", to receive-"catechetical instructions", and instruction in "easy, familiar explanatory questions upon the Church Catechism, and so through all plain and necessary things in a body of divinity".[8]

It seems to have been a training in content rather than method.

Fifty years later the Revd Thomas Charles, who towards the end of the eighteenth century revived the Circulating Schools in north Wales, chose his teachers with equal care, and not only gave them initial training but also inspected their work whenever he moved them from one district to another.

In the 1780s a training scheme was started at the school recently established by the Society of Friends (the Quakers) at Ackworth near Pontefract, in Yorkshire. Harassed by shortage of teachers, the governors resolved:

to engage two boys and two girls of suitable disposition and qualifications as apprentices until they attain twenty-one years.[9]

As has been seen, apprenticeship to teaching was no new idea. What renders the Ackworth scheme memorable is that for over a century it was "the backbone of the teaching profession in the Society of Friends".[10]

Perennial shortage of competent teachers was a main obstacle to the development of popular education in the eighteenth century. As the nineteenth century dawned, two men claimed, almost simultaneously, to have solved the problem: the Revd Dr Andrew Bell, an Anglican priest who had taught in India, and Joseph Lancaster, a young Quaker with no formal qualifications but a great love and some understanding of children.

Use pupils as teachers, they both said. Then, you will need only one adult, a 'Superintendent', for any school, however large. The Superintendent will teach selected scholars, and these, under his observant eye, will teach the rest. So easy! And so cheap! For, of course, the teacher-scholars, the 'Monitors', would not be paid.

Again, the idea was not new; but what *was* new was the systematic and detailed fashion in which it was worked out, especially by Lancaster, whose 'British' scheme was a masterpiece of intricate planning. Organisation, administration, curriculum, methodology, examination, discipline, welfare: each was broken down into small units, to be mastered by the Monitors, and by them passed on to the other pupils.

> The very essence of the system was the monitor ... When a child was admitted, a monitor assigned him to his class; while he remained, a monitor taught him (with nine other pupils); when he was absent, one monitor ascertained the fact, and another found out the reason; a monitor examined him periodically, and when he made progress, a monitor promoted him; a monitor ruled the writing paper; a monitor made or mended the pens; a monitor had charge of the slates and books; and a monitor-general looked after all the other monitors.[11]

Bell's 'Madras' system[12] was not so elaborate, but was nevertheless quite complicated.

For such systems to succeed, Monitors had to be trained. Though Lancaster protested that their duties were simple, the scrupulously accurate performance of these which he required could hardly be expected of barely literate children, some as young as seven and few more than twelve years old, without at least a modicum of training. Lancaster realised this, and made it the Superintendent's duty to ensure that monitors were not only "*able, as scholars,* to understand and perform the lessons they are appointed to teach", but also "*instructed,* under the inspection of the superintendent, in the mode of teaching".[13]

If Monitors needed training, even more so did Superintendents. They had to master the entire 'system', and then—all on their own—either start it in a new school, or (often a more difficult task) introduce it into a school hitherto taught on other lines.

In 1805, or possibly earlier, Lancaster began to carry out:

> a plan for training lads and young men as schoolmasters, by a practical knowledge of these improved modes of tuition, to be obtained in my institution, and under my own eye.[14]

A year or two later he invented the Teacher's Certificate—not least in order to protect his own reputation! In the preface to the 1808 edition of his book *Improvements in Education* he announced that:

> As to the practical *knowledge of this plan* (i.e. the 'British' system)

the public are desired to consider no person practically qualified to teach it, who have not a certificate from J Lancaster of their having been under his care. This will prevent the intrusion of imposters [*sic*] whose lame attempts only discredit the plan in the eyes of such as have not seen the original, or duly investigated its merits.[15]

For the students whom he selected for training Lancaster built a hostel alongside his school in the Borough Road of Southwark in south London; and thus established the first training college for teachers in the United Kingdom—still known in 1975 by the name of the street in which it was born, though it moved from there in 1890.

It is unlikely, though not impossible, that Bell was training teachers in England as early as 1805. In December 1804 Lancaster visited him, and, according to Bell, "interrogated me about my mode of training teachers".[16] But this questioning almost certainly concerned the training Bell had done in India. Bell in turn enquired about Lancaster's methods—and was singularly unimpressed. "Nothing was ever so burlesque," he wrote later to that ardent Anglican educationist, Mrs Sarah Trimmer, "as his forming his teachers by lectures on the Passions."

> It is by attending the school, seeing what is going on there, and taking a share in the office of tuition, that teachers are to be formed, and not by lectures and formal instruction.[17]

Thus early was born the barren dispute about the relative value of theory and practice in the training of teachers.

Lancaster's experiment in training seems to have been scholastically successful. Unfortunately, he could not manage money. In 1808 a small committee was formed to extricate him from his financial difficulties. In 1810 this committee was greatly enlarged, to look after 'The Institution for Promoting the Education of the Labouring and Manufacturing Classes of Society of every Religious Persuasion'. This title, which indicated the undenominational character of the Society, soon gave way to 'The Royal Lancasterian Institution'. In 1814, when Lancaster, after repeated quarrels, resigned, it became 'The British and Foreign School Society', the name it still bore in 1975.

Bell was concerned with the training of teachers by 1808, when, at the request of the Bishop of Durham, the Honourable Shute Barrington, he drafted a scheme for a school at Bishop Auckland which included a centre for training Monitors as Superintendents. The Barrington school was opened in 1810, and sent out its first trained Superintendent in the same year.

At the same time Bell was advocating a country-wide Church of England organisation to promote 'Madras' schools. He outlined his idea of this in 1808 in a pamphlet entitled *A Sketch of a National Institution for training up the Children of the Poor*. His idea gained influential support, and resulted in the foundation in 1811 of 'The National Society for Promoting the Education of the Poor in the Principles of the Established Church throughout England and Wales'.

Before the National Society was founded Bell had begun to urge the necessity of a school "in perfect order in the metropolis, where masters may be trained".[18] He had not long to wait; in 1812 the Society opened such a school in Baldwin's Gardens, off the Gray's Inn Road in central London. This was for twenty years thereafter the Society's main training centre. Others developed in diocesan 'Central' schools.

The rise of the two Societies institutionalised the sectarian differences between the two Monitorial systems; and unhappily, although both Societies were pursuing the same general aim, the religious and moral betterment of the children of the poor, their competitive rivalry effectively prevented a united national effort. This had a lasting effect upon the recruitment, training, and service of teachers in public Elementary schools.

When the British and National Societies assumed responsibility for the training of their teachers they were both shocked by the state of affairs they found. The National Society discovered that many applicants for training, including serving teachers, were "unable to write, and in some cases even to read". The Society resolved that:

> either a certificate of their having these qualifications must be required, or an examination by us take place before they are admitted to be trained.[19]

In 1813 the Society made a final examination and a period of probationary teaching obligatory before the award of the Teacher's Certificate. The probationary period was, admittedly, very short; it need not last more than one week. But the whole training course was ordinarily completed within a month or six weeks.

In 1814 the British and Foreign School Society responded to criticism of the training of teachers at Borough Road by appointing a 'Sub-committee on Schoolmasters' to investigate the matter. The sub-committee laid the blame on the training scheme, in which:

> no attempt has been made to teach the youths anything beyond the regular routine of school-training for children in general ... the greater part of the time, which might have been employed to increase their knowledge and improve their minds, has been lost, and habits of idleness rather encouraged.

"The degree of ignorance in which many of the youths have been sent out to form and conduct Schools," concluded the sub-committee, "has been such as to reflect discredit on the Institution." It recommended that henceforth the course should include:

> firstly, a knowledge of English grammar sufficient to qualify them to speak and write their own language with correctness and propriety; secondly, the improvement of their handwriting and knowledge of arithmetic; thirdly, geography and history, and in addition, when time and other circumstances will permit ... other useful branches of knowledge.[20]

The Society agreed, and thus—all unwittingly—stereotyped for generations the training college curriculum. Throughout the nineteenth century, and into the twentieth in some colleges, English grammar, arithmetic, history, geography, and handwriting made up its too, too solid core, around which were draped many and various (more or less) "useful branches of knowledge".

The earliest training courses were for men only. At Baldwin's Gardens this remained the case until 1815. There seems some doubt about when the training of women began at Borough Road; it could have been any time between 1808 and 1812. What is certain is that in 1812 Miss Ann Springman (later Mrs MacRae), who had been Lancaster's Monitor-General in 1806, was appointed head of the girls' school, and of an institution for training women teachers. Except during a period of ten years (1843–53) after her marriage, this remarkable woman—who has not yet received the notice she deserves—ruled the 'Female Department of the Training School' at

Borough Road until 1861, when it became a separate college, and moved to Stockwell in south-west London.

Before the 1840s there were no 'training colleges' in the modern sense. Teachers were trained in 'Model' schools, or in 'Centres' attached to schools. Borough Road was to some extent an exception to this generalisation; it was, in embryonic form but nevertheless recognisably, from the beginning a residential training college. But even twenty years after its foundation its students were spending 25 hours a week teaching in school, as against 23 scheduled hours of study.

The pioneers who in the 1840s created the English training college took over several important features which the training schools had evolved: an academic qualification for entry, a course comprising concurrently general education and professional training, a final examination, and a period of probationary teaching before the award of the Teacher's Certificate. They also adopted the principle that training colleges should be residential.

References

1 SPCK Minutes, 16 March 1698–99. Quoted from Jones, M G, *The Charity School Movement*, Cambridge University Press, 1938, p. 38.

2 *An Account of Charity Schools in Great Britain and Ireland*, SPCK, 1711, p. 50. Quoted from Sylvester, D W, *Educational Documents 800–1816*, Methuen, 1970, p. 175.

3 For complete lists of required qualifications see Jones, M G, op. cit. pp. 98–99.

4 Jones, M G, op. cit. p. 102.

5 Jones, M G, op. cit. p. 101. The words in inverted commas are from the Minutes of the St Martin's in the Fields (London) Charity School for Girls dated 15 November 1715.

6 Clarke, W K Lowther, *A History of the SPCK*, SPCK, 1958, p. 38.

7 The Model Schools were at Bath in Somerset, Blewbury in Berkshire, Artleborough and Findon in Northamptonshire.

8 Quoted from Professor Glanmor Williams's essay in *Pioneers of Welsh Education*, University College of Swansea Faculty of Education, 1965, p. 17.

9 Vipont, Elfrida, *Ackworth School*, Lutterworth Press, 1959, p. 42.

10 ibid.

11 Salmon, David, *Joseph Lancaster*, Longmans Green, for the British and Foreign School Society, 1904, p. 7.

12 Bell invented his Monitorial system while he was Superintendent of the Male Asylum (a school for soldiers' children) at Egremont near Madras in India. He says he used it as early as 1789.

13 Lancaster, J. *Improvements in Education, containing a complete epitome, of the system of education, invented and practised by the author.* Abridged edition, printed and sold by J Lancaster, Free School, Borough Road, Southwark, 1808, p. 8. (*Lancaster's italics.*)

14 Lancaster, op. cit., 3rd edition, 1805, p. 11.

15 Lancaster, op. cit., 1808 abridged edition, pp. vi–vii. (*Lancaster's italics.*)

16 Southey, R and C C, *The Life of Dr Bell*, John Murray, 1844, Vol. II, p. 127.

17 ibid., pp. 127 and 128.

18 ibid., p. 343. The quotation is from a letter by Bell written in August 1811.

19 ibid., p. 438.

20 British and Foreign School Society General Committee Minutes dated 7 May 1814. Quoted from Binns, H B, *A Century of Education:* Being the Centenary History of the British and Foreign School Society 1808–1908, Dent, 1908, p. 79.

CHAPTER TWO

Training Colleges

In 1837 there were only three establishments in England and Wales even remotely comparable with the Colleges of Education of the 1970s: Borough Road, the National Society's Training Centre at Westminster (moved from Baldwin's Gardens in 1832), and the recently opened Home and Colonial Infant School Society's Training Institution. By 1847 there were over twenty, and more on the way. All except Borough Road were associated with the Church of England.

The reasons why so rapid a growth took place are complicated, but they may be summarised as a struggle for power between the Church of England—the Established Church—and the Government. The Church was concerned to maintain its age-old claim to control and direct all education, the Government to introduce a novel, and still widely unaccepted, doctrine: that the State had not only the right, but also the duty, to play a part in the education of its citizens. The immediate victory was won, almost but not quite decisively, by the Church. This had fundamentally important consequences for Elementary education, and for the training of teachers for Elementary schools.

The question of who should train these teachers was among the first of the points at issue between Church and State to be determined. The battle about it had begun in earnest directly after the Reform Act of 1832, which brought into the House of Commons a number of members who were greatly perturbed by the grave defects in the country's provision for the health, housing, employment, and education of the great mass of working people.

In 1833 one of this group of would-be reformers, Mr A J Roebuck, a Radical who was MP for Bath, addressed the House at great length about the urgent necessity for a State system of education which would provide for "the universal and national Education of the whole People".[1] He failed to convince the Commons, but his plea was not entirely without effect. Eighteen days later the House (or a small number of its members) was induced to grant the sum of £20,000 in aid of the building of Public Elementary Schools in England and Wales. This was the first Parliamentary grant for public education in Great Britain, though Army education had been grant-aided since 1812.

In 1834 Lord Brougham, who had long campaigned for popular education, secured the appointment of a Select Committee of the House of Commons to inquire into its condition–as he had done previously with considerable effect. To this Committee he asserted, as he had done before, that it was the Government's duty to train teachers for Elementary schools; and he suggested that it should establish four Normal Schools, in London, Exeter, Lancaster, and York. The following year he again emphasised the necessity to train teachers, declaring that the most urgent need of popular education was for "seminaries where good schoolmasters might be trained".[2] His words evoked a quick response; within a few weeks the Home Secretary, Lord John Russell (a lifelong supporter of the British and Foreign School Society), persuaded the Commons to set aside £10,000, the sum Brougham had asked for, in aid of the building of Normal Schools. This was the first Parliamentary grant for the training of teachers in Britain, though not in the United Kingdom, for teacher-training in Ireland had been put on the grant list four years previously.

In February 1839 Lord John Russell, writing on behalf of the Queen, requested the Lord President of the Privy Council, Lord Lansdowne, to form "with four other of the Queen's servants ... a Board or Committee, for the consideration of all matters affecting the Education of the People".[3] In April a Committee of the Privy Council on Education was appointed; it consisted of the Lord President of the Council, the Lord Privy Seal, the Chancellor of the Exchequer, the Home Secretary, and the Master of the Mint. Immediately after its appointment it announced that it was going to establish a State Normal School for the training of Elementary School teachers.

The proposal evoked widespread protest, directed mainly against the arrangements for religious instruction. Anglicans objected to Nonconformists having a part in this (as was proposed), Nonconformists to the dominant role accorded to the Church of England. In June the Government 'postponed' the Normal School project. It was never revived. Even this admission of defeat did not placate the protesters, who through their Parliamentary representatives almost put an end to both the Committee of Council on Education and the Parliamentary grant for public education. The former was saved by five votes in a full House, the latter by only two.

When the state Normal School plan collapsed, the recently-appointed Secretary of the Committee of Council on Education, Dr James Phillips Kay—later Sir James Kay-Shuttleworth—took action on two fronts. As Secretary, he set himself to secure grants for voluntary training colleges. As a private individual he established with the aid of a friend, Mr E Carleton Tufnell, an experimental training college at Battersea, then a pretty village outside London.

Kay soon succeeded in getting capital grants for colleges, using first the £10,000 voted by Parliament in 1835. But it was not until 1846, when his pupil-teacher scheme was launched, that he got them maintenance grants.

Kay and Tufnell, who had studied training colleges in Scotland and Europe, hoped that theirs would blaze a trail in England. It did. Nearly a century later Dr R W Rich, the historian of nineteenth century training, declared that:

> Kay-Shuttleworth's experiment at Battersea is the most significant event in the history of the development of the English training college, for it was the type to which all subsequently founded training colleges conformed until the advent of the Day Training College. For good or for ill it established the residential college as the type.[4]

That possibly claims too much. Battersea was neither the first nor the only residential training college in England during the years 1840–43, when Kay and Tufnell were in charge of it. Borough Road had been residential for thirty years, and the Home and Colonial for three. The Chester Diocesan College, opened a few days before Battersea, had students in residence from October 1840. The National Society's first two colleges, St Mark's (men) and Whitelands (women), founded respectively in 1840 and 1841, were residential from the start. Some of the diocesan 'Central' schools, the earliest of which began training teachers in 1811, had provided residential accommodation for many years. It is better to regard Battersea as outstanding for other reasons. As Kay-Shuttleworth's biographer, Professor Frank Smith, said:

> it was an educational experiment on a large scale, where new methods of teaching were worked out, where continental reforms were adapted to English conditions, where text-books were prepared, and where methods of training teachers were tested and modified.[5]

Descriptions of the life and work at Battersea are given in most histories of English education. What is most important is to appreciate the aims and ideals of its founder. The key to understanding these is to realise that Kay-Shuttleworth (and Tufnell) thought of Elementary School teachers primarily as Christian missionaries. So their training had to be rooted in religion; "no skill can compensate adequately for the absence of a pervading religious influence on the character and conduct of schoolmasters".[6]

Not that Kay-Shuttleworth despised skill; on the contrary, he insisted upon high standards of scholastic knowledge and professional competence. What he hoped to cultivate in students was a harmonious combination of religious fervour, scholarly ardour for study, a high respect for professional expertise, and personal humility.

While Battersea undoubtedly played a leading part in creating the English training college, the contributions of others should not be overlooked or underestimated. That of Borough Road must have been considerable. The impact of David Stow's Glasgow Seminary was probably even greater than is ordinarily suggested. Chester developed original features. The Home and Colonial introduced notable innovations in both theory and practice. And there was the incalculable influence of St Mark's.

The first principal of St Mark's College, Chelsea, the Revd Derwent Coleridge (son of the poet Samuel Taylor Coleridge), was throughout his long reign (1841–64) the most controversial figure in the new world of the training college. He shared many of Kay-Shuttleworth's beliefs about teacher-training; especially that it should be conducted in a closely-knit residential community, devoted to unremitting endeavour, and dedicated to Christian aims. But he differed from him fundamentally on one crucial issue. Kay-Shuttleworth held that the primary purpose of a training college was to produce effective teachers, Coleridge that it was to nurture educated and cultured persons.

To this end Coleridge erected for his college elegant buildings, and created within them a community life designed to inspire and refine. Central to his concept was the college chapel, whose architectural beauty he enhanced by services of great dignity embellished by music of rare quality. Alongside the chapel he placed the college's 'Practising School'—built in the form of an Italian baptistery—as symbol that the school was the ante-chamber to the church.

Coleridge had in his day many critics, not least among Her Majesty's Inspectors of Schools (HMI). They had a point; the teachers he trained were some of them not such good practitioners as they should, and could, have been. But he introduced students to the idea of gracious living, taught them that education could bring both spiritual enrichment and social advance, and convinced many that teaching was not only a noble, but also a *learned*, profession.

St Mark's was one of some thirty training colleges in being by 1850. All except five were linked with the Church of England.[7] The British Society had opened colleges at Brecon (1845) and Bristol (1849),[8] and the Congregationalists two training schools in London, which were in 1852 to unite to form Homerton College.[9] In the near future, the Wesleyan Methodists were to open a men's college in Westminster, and the Roman Catholics one in Hammersmith.

All the colleges except one, Llandaff, were residential. All were, by modern standards, very small; in 1845 only Borough Road and the Home and Colonial had more than 100 students. None of the others exceeded 75.[10] Five claimed to provide three-year courses.[11] But nearly half did not pretend to keep students for more than one year, and several offered courses of six months, or less. The fact is that until the early 1850s, when 'Queen's Scholars' (the pick of the pupil-teachers) began to arrive, the colleges found students difficult to obtain, and still more difficult to retain for any length of time. Many students could not afford more than a brief stay. Many suffered from ill-health. Many were incapable of sustained study. Far too many suffered from all three disabilities.

The college staffs worked very hard to make something worthwhile out of such indifferent material. They gave their students inordinately long hours of study, on a vast range of subjects: typically, Religious Knowledge, Church History, English Grammar, English Literature, History, Geography, Arithmetic, Algebra, Geometry, Mensuration, Natural Philosophy (i.e. science), Handwriting, Drawing, Music, with occasionally some educational theory, and invariably much school practice. Inevitably, academic 'study' was reduced to information, memorisation, and regurgitation.

In many colleges the pressure of work, combined all too often with badly-cooked food and inferior accommodation, caused frequent breakdowns. Women suffered more than men. They had, in general, poorer buildings, poorer amenities, a poorer staff–student ratio, and heavier domestic duties. And they were more conscientious and compliant than the men.

Queen's Scholars began to arrive in 1852. They were to give the kiss of life to the colleges.

References

1 For Roebuck's speech see Hansard, 30 July 1833, Vol. XX, cols. 139–66.
2 Hansard, 21 May 1835. Vol. XXVII, col. 1332.
3 Lord John Russell's letter to Lord Lansdowne is reproduced in Maclure, J Stuart, *Educational Documents 1816–1963*, Chapman and Hall, 1965, pp. 42–45.
4 Rich, R W, *The Training of Teachers in England and Wales during the Nineteenth Century*, Cambridge University Press, 1933, p. 75.
5 Smith, Frank, *The Life and Work of Sir James Kay-Shuttleworth*, John Murray, 1923, p. 105.
6 From Kay-Shuttleworth's second report on Battersea. Reprinted in his *Four Periods of Public Education*, Longman Green, Longman and Roberts, 1862, p. 359.
7 Borough Road, Brecon and Bristol (British Society), and the two Congregational colleges.
8 The Brecon college was moved to Swansea in 1849, the Bristol college closed in 1852.
9 Homerton College took its name from the north London district in which it was located until 1894, when it moved to Cambridge.
10 Outside the jurisdiction of the Committee of Council on Education was the Army Normal School, established in 1846 in the Royal Military

Asylum at Chelsea, where training of Army schoolmasters had been started by Bell in 1812.

11 Bristol, St Mark's, Exeter, Salisbury, and York. The Church of England college at Warrington in Lancashire advertised a five-year course.

CHAPTER THREE

Pupil-Teachers

There is no doubt that in their early days the Monitorial schools were better than most other schools providing elementary education for the children of the poor. But gradually their limitations became obvious, and distasteful, to discriminating educators.

Among the dissatisfied was a young medical man, Dr J Phillips Kay, who after working in the slums of Manchester was, in 1835, appointed an Assistant Commissioner under the Poor Law Amendment Act of 1834, and posted to East Anglia. Part of his job there was to see that children resident in Poor Law 'workhouses'—institutions for aged, ailing, and other dependent paupers— got proper schooling. He was horrified by the appalling conditions in which many of these children were living, herded together with "adults whose brutish behaviour defied description,"[1] and taught—if taught at all—by some inmate detailed for the task.

His experiences led him to begin a series of epoch-making educational experiments. He visited Stow's Glasgow Seminary and Wood's Edinburgh Sessional School, recruited teachers from each, and set these to work in East Anglia as 'organising masters', that is, peripatetic teachers who travelled from one workhouse to another, trying to bring order and efficiency into their schools.

This first venture was not very successful. The Scottish teachers, with one exception, Richard Horne, later to be one of Kay's best assistants, could not endure the conditions, and left. Perhaps the chief benefit of the experiment was that it made Kay realise the magnitude of the enterprise he was essaying. Not a handful but a host of trained teachers was needed.

The story is often told of how in 1838 Kay found a fourteen-year-old boy, William Rush, running single-handed a workhouse school in the absence of the teacher through illness, and of how this incident turned his mind towards the idea of pupil-teachers. A charming anecdote, but surely not the whole truth? Kay had seen Monitors at work, he had seen *paid* Monitors, and had noted how much better they were than the unpaid. And from paid Monitors to pupil-teachers was, in principle, only a single logical step. Moreover, the use of pupil-teachers was no novelty in Europe.

What the incident may well have done was to induce Kay to visit Holland, where a statutory system of pupil-teaching had been in existence since 1816. He made two visits, and determined to try a similar scheme in England. An opportunity to experiment came in 1838, when he was transferred to London. He found in Norwood a large Poor Law school whose proprietor was prepared to co-operate, secured a grant of £500 from the Home Office, and reorganised the school. He ended Monitorial teaching, grouped the pupils in classes of forty, partitioned spaces to form classrooms, built workshops, rented a farm, acquired a naval instructor—and appointed some pupil-teachers.

> Boys and girls who reached the age of fourteen and were distinguished by "zeal, attainments and gentleness of disposition" were asked to stay on at Norwood in the capacity of assistant masters and mistresses ... they were paid a small salary, provided with extra tuition in the evenings, clothed in special uniforms and granted the privilege of sleeping in separate cubicles.[2]

Should that attractive description of Kay's first pupil-teachers conjure up in any reader's mind an impression of a rather cosy suburban boarding school, here, in his own words, is the stark reality.

> The pauper children at Norwood, from the garrets, cellars and wretched rooms of alleys and courts, in the dense parts of London, are often sent thither in a low state of destitution, covered only with rags and vermin; often the victims of chronic disease; almost universally stunted in their growth; and sometimes emaciated with want. The low-browed and inexpressive physiognomy or malign aspect of the boys is a true index

to the mental darkness, the stubborn tempers, the hopeless spirits, and the vicious habits, on which the master has to work.[3]

And on which Kay's fourteen-year-old pupil-teachers—distinguished by their "zeal, attainments and gentleness of disposition"—had to practise their 'prentice hands.

The experiment, which was highly successful, was to culminate eight years later in the national pupil-teacher scheme devised by Kay-Shuttleworth, and launched by the Committee of Council. In brief, the scheme was as follows:

1 Carefully selected Elementary school pupils, aged thirteen or more, who satisfied certain scholastic, moral, and physical conditions, would be apprenticed to equally carefully selected head teachers, for a period of five years.

2 They would teach throughout the school day, and would be taught by the head before or after school hours, for at least one hour and a half on each of five days a week.

3 They would be examined annually by HMI.

4 They would be paid by the Committee of Council. Boys would get £10 for the first year, and rise by annual increments of £2 10s. (£2.50) to a maximum of £20. Girls would get about two-thirds of these amounts.

5 These salaries would be paid by the Committee of Council "irrespective of other sums that may be received from the school or from any other source".

6 The head teachers would be paid for supervising and teaching their pupil-teachers: £5 a year for one, £9 for two, and £3 each for others, up to a maximum of £15 a year; with additional payments for instruction in 'practical' subjects such as gardening and laundrywork.

7 A head's remuneration was conditional upon his pupil-teacher(s) securing at HMI's annual examination "a certificate of good character and satisfactory progress".

8 Pupil-teachers could be employed at the ratio of one to every 25 pupils on roll.

9 A pupil-teacher, on completing successfully his apprenticeship, would receive from the Committee of Council a certificate which entitled him to:

(i) sit a public examination, to be held annually, for the award of 'Queen's Scholarships'. These would qualify their holders for places in recognised training colleges, with annual maintenance grants of £25 for men, and £20 for women; *or*

(ii) take a post in a grant-aided Elementary school as an 'Uncertificated Teacher'; *or*

(iii) take a post in one of the "departments of state which have hitherto been the objects of purely political patronage"—which meant in fact some of the lower clerical grades in the Civil Services. (This option was withdrawn in 1852.)

10 Training college students who successfully completed one, two, or three years' training would be awarded, respectively, a first-class, second-class, or third-class Teacher's Certificate. This Certificate would entitle the holder to an annual supplement to his/her salary, at the rate of £15 to £20 for a first-class Certificate, £20 to £25 for a second-class, and £25 to £30 for a third-class. Payment of these supplements by the Committee of Council was subject to three conditions:

(i) that the school managers paid the teacher a salary of at least double the supplement, and

(ii) provided the teacher with a rent-free house;

(iii) that HMI certified that the teacher's "character, conduct, and attention to his duties" were satisfactory, and that the school was efficient.

11 There was a rather vague promise that the Committee of Council would make supplementary grants in aid of pensions for teachers. (This promise, never satisfactorily redeemed, was for years a cause of misunderstanding and dispute.)

12 The Committee of Council would make grants to recognised (i.e. inspected) training colleges in respect of *all* their students (Queen's Scholars were not to number more than a quarter of the annual intake): £20 for a student who successfully

completed one year's training, £25 for one who completed two years, and £30 for one who completed three. (Regrettably, the Committee forgot to include in this spate of generosity any additional remuneration for the teachers in the training colleges—some of whom soon found that they were being paid less than some of their students! This anomaly was rectified in 1851.)

It is essential to realise that Kay-Shuttleworth never intended pupil-teaching to be a self-sufficient means of training. It was only the first stage. Pupil-teachers would "complete their training ... by passing through the course of discussion and instruction provided in a Normal School".[4] Unfortunately, this vital part of the scheme went astray from the start, because (1) many pupil-teachers did not attempt to enter a Normal School, and (2) the Teacher's Certificate was made available to serving teachers by examination, without Normal School training.

During the early years of the pupil-teacher scheme HMI—who chose the entrants—were many of them almost lyrical in its praise. "Every successive year," wrote the Revd Muirhead Mitchell in 1851, "only increases the conviction of myself, with all the managers and clergy, that the pupil-teacher system was one of the most valuable inventions, for its purpose, that was ever devised."[5] Mr T W M Marshall, inspector for Roman Catholic schools, was more down to earth, but hardly less enthusiastic. He declared in 1852 that:

> even the least successful amongst them [the pupil-teachers] has proved far more useful and efficient than the best of the incompetent and unsalaried 'monitors' whom they have super-seded.[6]

Euphoria about pupil-teachers did not last very long—and there were some doubters from the start. But with all its imperfections, the pupil-teacher system undoubtedly improved both the efficiency and the morale of the schools, as its predecessor, the monitorial system, had done in its heyday.

References

1 Pollard, H M *Pioneers of Popular Education*, John Murray, 1956, p. 216.
2 ibid., p. 231.
3 Kay-Shuttleworth, Sir James, *Four Periods of Public Education*, pp. 295–96.

4 *The School in its relation to the State, the Church, and the Congregation*, p. 36. This pamphlet, published anonymously in 1847 in defence of the Government's record in Elementary education, was written by Kay-Shuttleworth, probably at the request of the Committee of Council. He reprinted it in *Four Periods of Public Education* (pp. 471–93).

5 *Minutes of the Committee of Council on Education 1850–51*, Vol. II, p. 268.

6 *Minutes of the Committee of Council on Education 1851–52*, Vol. II, pp. 524–25.

CHAPTER FOUR

Reverse and Revival

Until 1853 the training colleges were not allowed to offer more than a quarter of their places to Queen's Scholars. Consequently, most were not full, many of their students were mediocre, or worse, and their educational standards remained low.

Realising this, the Committee of Council began in 1853 a series of reforms. It ended the limitation on the number of Queen's Scholars a college could accept, and made the renewal of scholarships for a second year automatic for students who passed the first year examination. It offered allowances of £100 a year to resident lecturers (one, two, or three of them, according to the size of the college) who had above average attainments in one or two subjects, to be chosen from English Literature, History, Geography, Applied Mathematics, and Physical Science. And it made a determined effort to standardise the length of the college course, and to introduce a common curriculum. In 1854 the Revd Henry Moseley, HMI, undertook to draft a syllabus, and produced one based on three principles:

1 Not to add to or take from the existing subjects of the examination.

2 To give the greatest weight to the subjects of Elementary education.

3 Not to attempt to do more than could be done well.[1]

The Committee of Council accepted the syllabus, and told the colleges that their examinations would in future be based upon it.

Moseley's syllabus covered three years, but to expect many students to remain so long was unrealistic. The Committee of Council concentrated its efforts on attracting Queen's Scholars into the colleges, and inducing them to stay for two years. It had a large measure of success; by 1859 more than five out of six students were Queen's Scholars, and the unsatisfactory private student had been virtually eliminated.

But by this time other troubles were beginning to cast a shadow over the colleges. Queen's Scholars were not all proving academically élite; on the contrary, many were ill-educated and ignorant. A common syllabus and examination was not proving wholly a blessing; in particular, it gave the Committee of Council, acting through its newly established Education Department, too much influence. The appointment in 1856 of a Vice-President of the Committee of Council, to be responsible to the House of Commons for public education, was largely inspired by a demand for national economy evoked by the cost of the Crimean war. A Royal Commission (the 'Newcastle' Commission) which had been appointed in 1858 to discover how "sound and cheap" elementary education could be expanded, was asking disconcerting questions about cost-effectiveness.

The colleges felt themselves to be financially very vulnerable. The cost of the pupil-teacher scheme, on which they depended for their students, had almost quadrupled between 1851 and 1857, from £150,000 to £540,000. The most efficient colleges, because they got excellent results in the annual examinations, were making 75 to 90 per cent of their income from Parliamentary grants.

Their fears were realised. In 1859 the Committee of Council restricted the number of pupil-teachers a school might have. In 1860 it announced that it would not consider "any new applications for grant towards the expense of building, enlarging, improving, or fitting up training colleges".[2] In 1862 the Vice-President, Mr Robert Lowe, imposed his notorious 'Revised Code of Regulations'; it was for some years to harm the colleges almost as much as the schools.

The Revised Code abolished specific grants to schools, and substituted a single block grant, payable to the managers. Among the grants abolished were those for pupil-teachers' salaries and teachers' fees for educating pupil-teachers. As pupil-teachers had to be paid out of the block grant, managers naturally got them as cheaply as they could; and the average salaries paid to pupil-teachers dropped significantly. This, together with the replacement of five-year indentured apprenticeships by contracts renewable every six months, caused a sharp decline in the number of entrants into pupil-teaching: from 3,092 in 1862 to 1,895 in 1867. Concurrently, the quality of applicants worsened, and so did in many cases that of the education given to pupil-teachers.

In 1863 Queen's Scholarships were abolished. So was the system of paying *per capita* grants on examination successes. Henceforth these were to be paid only on students who had spent two full years in college, passed their examinations, and completed satisfactorily their period of probationary teaching. Moreover, the total grant to a college was not to exceed 75 per cent of its annual expenditure. Finally, adding insult to injury, the Committee of Council abolished the three grades of Teacher's Certificate based on one, two, or three years' training. It substituted four grades, of which the colleges could award only the lowest. The others would be awarded by HMI to serving teachers, with minimum intervals of five years between grades.

These measures hit the men's colleges hard; their numbers fell from 1,167 in 1863 to 860 in 1865. Two small colleges closed: Highbury and Chichester. The large mixed college at Cheltenham, which had for years lived almost entirely on Government grants, was saved from bankruptcy only by the proceeds of the sale of the Highbury property. The women's colleges were little affected; there were few other occupations open to educated women, the colleges were cheaper to run, and the demand for women teachers strong: they accepted lower salaries than men.

Mercifully, the depression did not last very long; the Elementary Education Act 1870 transformed the situation. Many more teachers were required. Unfortunately, the Act did not give School Boards the power to train them. The voluntary bodies did what they could. The British Society doubled the number of its student places in three years, expanding Borough Road and Stockwell, and opening in 1872 women's colleges at Darlington and Swansea. The Church of England opened colleges at Chichester and Oxford in 1872 and at Tottenham in 1874. The Roman Catholics opened in 1874 a college in Wandsworth.

These efforts were insufficient to cope with a school population which doubled between 1870 and 1876. The Committee of Council resorted to various expedients to increase the supply of teachers. It restored grants on examination results, and the title of 'Queen's Scholar'. It allowed colleges to pass out students after one year's training; in 1873 nearly half of the Westminster students (57 out of 124) who left were one-year trained. It gave HMI power to recommend, without examination, serving teachers for the Certificate; between 1871 and 1874 over 3,000 teachers were thus Certificated. It lowered the pass standard for the Certificate.

The number of Certificated teachers nearly trebled between 1870 and 1880: from 12,467 to 31,422. The number of pupil-teachers more than doubled: from 14,612 to 32,128 (the Committee of Council reduced its grant to schools which did not employ a specified number). The fastest proportionate growth was of 'Assistant' teachers, that is, ex-pupil-teachers who did not have the Certificate: from 1,262 to 7,652. Within a few years the number of uncertificated teachers was to exceed in many areas the number of the Certificated. This growth was due partly to the general demand for teachers, but more particularly to the fact that many small School Boards, and a great number of Voluntary school managers, went shopping in the cheapest market.

The growing number of uncertificated teachers made many people fear that the quality of elementary education would deteriorate. But the greater threat to quality was the increasing number of pupil-teachers. Far from being regarded as the saviours of the schools, as they had been twenty years previously, pupil-teachers were in the 1870s widely felt to be lowering their standards. To improve matters the Liverpool and London School Boards began to gather their pupil-teachers into classes for their education. The practice spread rapidly in the areas of the larger urban School Boards; in these, by 1890 most pupil-teachers were being educated in Pupil-Teacher Centres.

The value of these Centres was enhanced by other measures. In 1875 the London School Board raised the age of entry into pupil-teaching in its area to fifteen for boys, and in 1881 for girls also. In 1884 it abolished compulsory education outside school hours for its pupil-teachers, reduced their hours of teaching to three a day, and required their attendance at a Pupil-Teacher Centre for five sessions a week, all within school hours. Liverpool did the same for first-year pupil-teachers. The Committee of Council was forced—reluctantly—

to follow suit. In 1878 it raised the national age of admission into pupil-teaching to fourteen. But it did not raise it to fifteen; that was not to come until 1900.

Between 1886 and 1888 both pupil-teacher and training college systems were put under the microscope by a Royal Commission (the 'Cross' Commission),[3] appointed "to inquire into the working of the Elementary Education Acts, England and Wales". The Commission produced Majority and Minority Reports. About pupil-teaching these differed fundamentally. The Majority asserted that:

> having regard to moral qualifications, there is no other available, or as we prefer to say, equally trustworthy source from which an adequate supply of teachers is likely to be forthcoming.[4]

They consequently recommended that:

> with modifications, tending to the improvement of their education, the apprenticeship of pupil-teachers ... ought to be upheld.[5]

The Minority declared that:

> In general we consider that the pupil-teacher system is now the weakest part of our educational machinery, and that great changes are needed in it if it is to be continued.[6]

During the 1890s opinion among teachers and educational administrators tended increasingly to agree with the Minority. In 1896 the Committee of Council appointed a Departmental Committee, under the chairmanship of the Revd T W Sharpe, Senior Chief Inspector, "to inquire into the workings of the Pupil-Teacher system". Reporting in 1898, the members of this committee showed themselves keenly aware of the weaknesses of the system. "We wish to record as emphatically as possible," they wrote at the beginning of their report:

> our conviction that the too frequent practice of committing the whole of the training and teaching of classes to immature and uneducated young persons is economically wasteful and educationally unsatisfactory, and even dangerous, to the teachers and taught in equal measure.[7]

Nevertheless, the committee did not propose abolishing the system, because "some sort of pupilage or apprenticeship is undoubtedly of the highest value." Moreover:

> for the present, the system is established so firmly in the economy of national education that it would be impossible, even if ... desirable, to sweep it away, or to make any violent and revolutionary changes.[8]

So the Committee contented themselves with advocating reforms. They felt that the existing Pupil-Teacher Centres were not good enough, because they could not, "under present conditions, adequately fulfil the purposes of secondary schools", and so give the secondary education which all pupil-teachers should have. But they foresaw a bright future for the best of the Centres.

> We look forward to the ultimate conversion of those centres which are well staffed and properly equipped into real secondary schools, where, although perhaps intending teachers may be in the majority, they will have ampler time for their studies, and will be instructed side by side with pupils who have other careers in view.[9]

That conversion was to take place perhaps rather sooner than the Committee expected.

References

1 Letter from the Revd Henry Moseley to the Lord President of the Council dated 2 May 1854. Reproduced in *Minutes of the Committee of Council 1854-55*, pp. 14–22.
2 Minute of the Committee of Council dated 21 January 1860.
3 Chairman, Sir Richard Assheton Cross. When the Commission was appointed he was Home Secretary. A few months later he was made Secretary of State for India, and given a peerage.
4 Cross Commission Final Report, Part III, Chapter 5, p. 88.
5 ibid.
6 ibid., p. 242.
7 *Report of the Departmental Committee on the Pupil-Teacher System*, Her Majesty's Stationery Office (HMSO), 1898, p. 4.
8 ibid.
9 ibid., p. 8.

CHAPTER FIVE

Aid from Universities

Among the matters which the Cross Commission was asked to inquire into was the possibility of establishing in England and Wales non-residential 'Day Training Colleges', like those in Scotland. This inquiry had been strongly urged by some of the large School Boards, not only because of the absolute shortage of training college places, but also because well over two-thirds of the existing places, being in church colleges, were reserved for members of particular religious denominations.

It was also widely felt that the residential colleges were introverted, unprogressive, obsessed with examinations, and out of touch with the schools. In fairness to the colleges it must be said that by themselves they could do little about most of their limitations. Most of the church colleges were compelled by their trust deeds to admit only members of their own denomination. Without capital grants (and the colleges had had none for nearly thirty years), the enlargement or improvement of premises was difficult. As much of the colleges' income depended upon good examination results, staffs had to concentrate upon success in the examinations leading to the Teacher's Certificate—examinations, incidentally, which they neither set nor marked, and based on syllabuses they did not prepare. So inadequately educated were many of their entrants that rote instruction was the only means of getting them up to pass standard in time. (Many members of staff, having been appointed directly their student days ended, knew no other method.)

College staffs still believed in long hours of study and teaching; at St Hild's, the women's college at Durham, for example, the students of 1877 got 46 hours a week of "public lessons and lectures", and had also to do "private study and industrial work"—the latter a euphemism for domestic duties.[1] At Bede, the men's college, in 1887 students were getting 38¼ hours of class teaching and 17½ hours of private study.

The curriculum consisted almost exclusively of academic subjects, among which psychology, or 'the principles of learning', found a place in some colleges. Students spent several hours a week observing or teaching in the college's 'Demonstration', or 'Practising' school, and once a week endured the dreaded ritual of the 'criticism lesson', when they taught classes in front of their fellow students and the staff, and were publicly criticised by them.

The annual examinations were in two Parts: 1, Professional Subjects; 2, Academic. Part 1 included Reading and Recitation, School Management, and (second year only) Teaching a Class. Women students were also examined in Needlework and Domestic Economy, and any student could offer Music. Part 2 comprised a core of compulsory subjects and a long list of optional. The compulsory subjects were English Language and Literature, English History, Geography, Arithmetic, and Mathematics. Among the optional were half a dozen foreign languages, the physical and biological sciences, and political economy. Most students prepared themselves for examination by memorising lecture notes and passages from textbooks, a method which had one merit only: there were few failures. In 1882 there was none.

From 1873 training colleges could enter students for the examinations of the Department of Science and Art. As success earned prizes for candidates and grants for their teachers, these examinations became hugely popular in the colleges, some of which made substantial incomes from them.

Students had little time for recreation, and few amenities to help them to enjoy it. Common rooms were rare; at Borough Road, for example, the classrooms and a small yard were the only places available for leisure pursuits. Libraries were very small, and often stocked mainly with unreadable books, the throw-outs from benefactors' shelves. Student Unions did not exist. Women's colleges were in general worse off than men's; students were more closely supervised, did more housework, and often got their only outdoor exercise in formal walks 'in crocodile'.

Despite their shortcomings, the colleges were stoutly defended, not least by HMI, before the Cross Commission. The Revd T W Sharpe, Senior Chief Inspector, who had previously been HMI for the men's colleges, said that they were doing "efficient work with a sufficient staff of teachers and with a carefully drawn syllabus of study"[2] ('drawn', incidentally, by HM Inspectorate).

The question of non-residential colleges proved highly controversial. "I should deplore the adoption of day training colleges in England," declared the Revd J P Norris, Archdeacon of Bristol, who had had long experience both as HMI and as diocesan inspector,

> a training college ought to be a home; you ought to have the students all through the twenty-four hours in order to form their personal habits.[3]

Equally strong arguments were advanced in favour of day training colleges. Professor H (later Sir Henry) Jones, principal of the recently founded University College at Bangor, went so far as to assert that they were "the only hope of elevating the schools".[4]

Mr J G (later Sir Joshua) Fitch, formerly principal of Borough Road, and now HMI for the women's colleges, probably expressed accurately the median point of view. Non-residential colleges, he thought, might very well prove to be of great service.

> They will be defective, no doubt, in the discipline and in some of the moral influences which belong now to the [residential] training colleges, and which are very valuable, but I think that they may give in some respects a broader and more liberal training.[5]

The Majority report of the Cross Commission recommended that a modest experiment be tried.

> Considering the demand that already exists for more ample or more generally available opportunities for training, and the importance of giving every facility for training to those who now obtain certificates without it; considering further, that such schemes as those submitted to us would, in their nature, be tentative, that they would not involve a large outlay of capital, and would only be adopted when local circumstances seemed to invite the adaptation of some existing educational machinery to

ST. PATRICK'S COLLEGE LIBRARY

this purpose, we think it might be well that some such experiment should be made, subject to the condition, that only a limited number of students should receive Government assistance towards their training.[6]

The Minority thought that the schemes which had been submitted deserved "a much heartier support".[7] It could hardly have been less hearty!

The Government accepted the Majority's recommendation. It sanctioned the establishment of day training colleges by universities and university colleges—but not by School Boards, though these had been foremost in advocating them. The colleges were not to admit, altogether, more than 200 Queen's Scholars; their curricula had to be approved by the Education Department; and they would be inspected by HMI. But one extremely important right was granted to their students; they could if they wished take an undergraduate course instead of Part II of the Department's course. The Department safeguarded its position by requiring that it see the syllabuses, examination papers and scripts, and the marks awarded.

A principal purpose of this arrangement was to enable training college students to study concurrently for a degree and the Teacher's Certificate. This was not unknown; in one or two colleges at any rate ambitious students had for some years been attempting the dual task. But it was an arduous business, and it involved additional work for staff as well as students, because of the difference between the certificate and degree syllabuses. The option of taking a university course, which was shortly offered to residential college students as well, was an attempt to lighten both loads. It did not, however, overcome the difficulty presented by the fact that degree courses lasted three years, certificate courses only two. So the Education Department asked the universities to specify:

> the extent to which the two years' attendance and the certificate of a student in training will count as part of a qualification for a university degree.[8]

Unfortunately, this attempt to institute a 'credit' system failed. So in 1891 the Department included in its Regulations a clause enabling students to spend a third year in college.[9] In 1893, to assist students of foreign languages, it allowed this year to be spent out of college.[10]

Borough Road and Stockwell immediately began to send students to France.

The universities and university colleges seized eagerly the opportunity to establish teacher training departments (they were not, strictly speaking, *colleges*). They opened six in 1890, another four in 1891, and four more in 1892. By 1900 there were sixteen, containing over 1,150 students, nearly a quarter of the total number (5,200) in training. This rapid development was not due entirely to zeal for education. To institutions that were desperately short of money, as most of the university colleges were, a regular supply of students paid for out of public funds must have seemed like manna from heaven.

One can hardly exaggerate the importance of the introduction of day training colleges. They increased substantially the supply of trained teachers for Public Elementary schools, ended the isolation of the training colleges and the near-monopoly of teacher training by religious denominations, gave the study of education academic status, and raised the prestige of the Elementary school teacher. Not least, they effected something like a revolution in the residential colleges, which they stimulated (or scared) into improving their accommodation, recruiting better staff, and humanising their regimes.

Their coming brought also, unfortunately, one unhappy consequence. They were established to train teachers for Elementary schools; but the possibility of their training also teachers for Secondary schools had been foreseen. This could have provided a prime opportunity for fusing the training of all teachers into a harmonious unity; and as they began to open secondary departments it seemed for a while that it might happen. "We rejoice to see," wrote the official Visitors to the university colleges in 1896, "that in many instances":

> these [university] colleges have drawn around them the Denominational Colleges and Seminaries of the district, and that the students of these institutions are receiving much of their instruction in the general classes and associating freely with, and partaking in the life of, the students of the University College.[11]

Alas! this promising venture into partnership did not last. Day training and residential colleges drew apart, and within the day training colleges the Elementary and Secondary departments became

// independent units. Thus the gap between Elementary and Secondary education was enlarged by segregating the training of their teachers.

References

1 Lawrence, Angel, *St Hild's College 1858–1958,* published by the College, 1958, p. 26. In the nineteenth century it was the normal practice in women's colleges, and in some of the men's, for the students to do most of the housework.

2 Cross Commission Final Report, 1888, p. 94.

3 Cross Commission 3rd Report, 1887, p. 183.

4 ibid., p. 322.

5 ibid., p. 550.

6 Cross Commission Final Report, p. 101.

7 ibid., p. 243.

8 Education Department Circular Letter No. 287, dated 27 May 1890, Section XIV (g).

9 *Code of Regulations for Public Elementary Schools 1891,* Article 120.

10 *Code of Minutes of the Education Department 1893,* Article 120.

11 *Report to the Committee on Grants to University Colleges in Great Britain 1896,* p. 4. The Visitors were Mr T H Warren, President of Magdalen College, Oxford, and Professor G D Liveing, Fellow of St John's College, Cambridge.

CHAPTER SIX

Delayed Action

The training of teachers for Secondary schools did not really get off the ground until the last quarter of the nineteenth century, though isolated instances occurred earlier. The Quaker school at Ackworth (previously mentioned), and the Woodard school at Hurstpierpoint, founded in 1849, had their own training schemes. Mrs Frances Buss, mother of the eminent headmistress Frances Mary Buss, along with others induced the Home and Colonial College in 1845 to take up the training of teachers for Secondary (or, more accurately, 'middle-class') schools. Later, Frances Mary was to send the members of her staff there to be trained.

Miss Buss became in 1870 the first woman member of the Council of the College of Preceptors. In 1873 she and Miss Beata Doreck (the second member) persuaded that body to start training classes for Secondary school teachers, under the direction of Joseph Payne, created in that year the first Professor of Education in the United Kingdom.

The most imaginative training scheme of the nineteenth century was that developed by Miss Dorothea Beale at the Cheltenham Ladies College, of which she became Principal in 1858. Whether she conceived the original idea seems uncertain. A friend of hers, Miss Margaret Newman, opened at Cheltenham in 1876 (at her own expense) a teacher training establishment for girls of slender means who wished to teach in Secondary schools. Unfortunately, Miss Newman died the following year, but Miss Beale ensured that her enterprise continued. She made a successful appeal for funds; these enabled her immediately to move the training institution into a larger house, and in 1885 to build in Cheltenham a residential training college, St Hilda's, and to buy in Oxford three acres of land, on which one day St Hilda's students would be able to do part of their study (which included degree courses) within the ambit of Britain's oldest university. St Hilda's, Oxford, was opened in 1893 (though not on the site Miss Beale had bought), and in 1898 was made a Hall of the University.

Miss Beale created also two other teacher training departments at the Ladies College, one for *Kindergarten* teachers, and one for "the training of cultured ladies as teachers in Elementary schools". Both remained in being for some time after her death in 1906. St Hilda's, Cheltenham, continued until 1925.

Meanwhile, Miss Buss was concerned with various training projects. In 1877 she became a member of 'The Teachers' Training and Registration Society', founded in that year by the sisters Emily Shirreff and Mrs Maria Grey. The Society opened in 1878 Bishopsgate Training College (renamed in 1885 Maria Grey college), which claimed to be "the first college in England to train women for teaching in secondary schools".[1] In 1885 she played a prominent part in the founding of the Cambridge Training College for Women, later to be called Hughes Hall, after its first principal, Miss E P Hughes.

In the north of England a very different venture was in the making. In 1887 Miss Charlotte Mason, who had been a teacher in Secondary school and Training college, drew up for a group of friends in Bradford "a scheme for a parents' educational union" which comprised "both a method of home education and a training for teachers".[2] In 1891 Miss Mason opened at Ambleside in the Lake District a 'House of Education' for the training of women as nurses or teachers who would serve in the homes of members of the Parents' Educational Union. (The training of nurses was later dropped.) On Miss Mason's death in 1923 the House of Education was renamed the Charlotte Mason College. It remained an independent institution until 1960, when it was transferred to the Westmorland County Council.

While the women acted, the men talked. The Schools Inquiry Commission discussed the training of Secondary school teachers, and decided against it. The Headmasters Conference, founded in 1869, debated the topic at most of its annual meetings in the 1870s. In 1875 Sir James Kay-Shuttleworth, now in his seventies but still eagerly interested in education, assembled a joint committee, representative of the public schools, the training colleges, and HM Inspectorate, and got it to issue a declaration in favour of training. The Headmasters Conference thereupon asked the Universities of Oxford and Cambridge to consider providing facilities for training Secondary school teachers. Oxford refused. Cambridge agreed, and established in 1879 a teacher training Syndicate. Women's training colleges made considerable use of the Syndicate's services; men virtually ignored them.

Two attempts to provide training colleges for men failed dismally. In 1883 a group of public school heads sponsored a college in London; it attracted so few students that it lasted only three years. A college opened in 1895 by the College of Preceptors had an even shorter life; it closed after two years. "Secondary training for male teachers," lamented the College of Preceptors' history published in 1896, "has not yet been accepted as a matter of course or necessity."[3]

Other initiatives had better fates. In 1883 London University, and in 1894 the Victoria University of Manchester, instituted postgraduate Diplomas in Education. In the 1890s eight day training colleges opened Secondary departments. In 1895 a Royal Commission on Secondary Education (the 'Bryce' Commission) came down, cautiously, in favour of training. And in 1897 a conference representative of all the Secondary school teachers' associations except the Headmasters Conference discussed, not whether but how, the training of teachers for Secondary schools should be conducted. They opted for a consecutive pattern: three years of study leading to a degree, followed by one year of professional training. This became, and has remained, the standard pattern.

References

1 London University Institute of Education Calendar 1975–76, p. 179. The claim could be made, however, for St Hilda's, Cheltenham.
2 Cholmondeley, Essex, *The Story of Charlotte Mason (1842–1923)*, Dent, 1960, p. 16.
3 *Fifty Years of Progress in Education*, The College of Preceptors, 1896, p. 38.

CHAPTER SEVEN

Training Specialists

The earliest specialist teachers in Britain were those who taught very young children. In Robert Owen's school their methods were different from those of teachers of older children. David Stow gave them a different training, and so did the Home and Colonial Society. The differences became more marked when in the 1850s the Baroness Marenholtz von Bülow introduced Froebel's *Kindergarten* into England.

The *Kindergarten* impressed many people favourably. Dickens praised it. So did HMI. The Revd Muirhead Mitchell wrote in his 1854 report that:

> This system, though intellectual, is truly infantile; it treats the child as a child; encourages him to think for himself; teaches him, by childish toys and methods, gradually to develop in action or hieroglyphic writing his own idea, to tell his own story and to listen to that of others . . . whatever is said and whatever is done is totally and altogether such as belongs to a child.[1]

Training colleges took it up. In 1857 the Home and Colonial Society asked Professor Heinrich Hoffman, a German Froebelian, to undertake the training of students in their college. In 1864 the British and Foreign School Society established a *Kindergarten* in the Infant school attached to its new training college for women at Stockwell. In 1874 this college invited Fraulein Eleanore Heerwart, a distinguished German teacher, to give a three months' series of lectures; she stayed for ten years, and did much to enhance the reputation of the *Kindergarten* in England.

In 1872 a Froebel training college was opened in Manchester, where shortly afterwards a Froebel Society was formed. In 1874 a London *Kindergarten* Society followed, and was supported by many of the most able protagonists of women's education. In the same year the London School Board appointed Miss M E Bishop, a member of the Society, as instructor to its Infant teachers. In 1880 the London and Manchester Societies went jointly in deputation to the Vice-President of the Committee of Council, Mr A J Mundella, to urge him to introduce the *Kindergarten* method into all Public Elementary schools. Mundella refused to go so far as that, but he inserted in the Elementary School Code the provision that Infant schools wishing to qualify for the new 'Merit' grant[2] must include in their curriculum "simple lessons on objects and the phenomena of nature and common life," with appropriate 'occupations'.

In 1879 the London Froebel Society opened a *Kindergarten* training college and school, with Miss Bishop as principal. In 1884 the Society, which had been holding examinations for *Kindergarten* teachers since 1876, instituted two Certificates: Lower, for assistant teachers, and Higher, for teachers aspiring to be heads of *Kindergartens*. In 1892 the Education Department recognised these certificates as approved qualifications for Elementary school teachers. In 1895 the endeavours of nearly half a century were crowned by the opening, in West Kensington, of the Froebel Educational Institute, designed to be the exemplar in England and Wales of *Kindergarten* training.

Domestic Subjects

Some of the most enlightened training of the nineteenth century took place in the Schools of Cookery established between 1873 and 1894 by "practically minded women citizens" to help the poor to choose and cook food well. The leaders of this movement, who selected staff and students with the greatest care, decided from the start to train their teachers, and exacted from trainees very high standards of proficiency. To secure their 'Full Teacher's Diploma', which covered 'High Class', 'Household', and 'Artisan' cooking, candidates had to pass three written examinations and three practical tests. To get a first-class pass they had to score 80 per cent on each.

In 1893 the Education Department gave its blessing to this business-like contribution to national education and welfare by issuing its first *Regulations for the Training of Teachers of Domestic Subjects*. Unfortunately, it did not offer the normal teacher-training grant, but only the much smaller grant for technical courses. This injustice was not rectified until 1906; before then, several Schools of Cookery had been forced by shortage of funds to give up training teachers.

Physical Education

The training of women as specialist teachers of physical education was begun in England by a Swedish woman of rare genius, Miss Martina Bergman. A graduate of the *Kongl Gymnastica Centralinstitutet* (Royal Central Gymnastic Institute) at Stockholm, then under the direction of Hjalmar Fredrik Ling, son of the founder, Per Hendrik Ling, she came to England in 1881 at the invitation of the London School Board, which appointed her its 'Superintendent of Physical Education in Girls' and Infants' Schools'.[3] She attacked her work with such enthusiasm and skill that within six years she had trained over 1,300 teachers, and thus enabled the girls in every London Elementary school to receive physical education.

Miss Bergman became convinced that physical education was as necessary in Secondary as in Elementary schools. So, in 1885, "with no other capital than her dreams and capacity for work",[4] she opened in Hampstead a private training school, offering to young middle-class women a two-year course which included anatomy, animal physiology, chemistry, physics, hygiene, and theory of movement, along with Ling gymnastics, swimming, and organised outdoor games. The last was a concession to English idiosyncrasy; games had no part in the Ling programme.

Women with a certificate from Madame Bergman-Österberg (as she became in 1886) were soon securing posts in Secondary schools in Britain and abroad. Women's colleges adopted her scheme: Bedford, Maria Grey, and Whitelands in London, Girton and Newnham at Cambridge. In 1887 Madame resigned from her School Board post to devote herself entirely to training women as specialist teachers of physical education. In 1895, having outgrown the Hampstead premises, she moved to Dartford in Kent. Here, with ample playing fields, outdoor games flourished: in the first year, cricket, lawn tennis, and "the new game of hockey", and later, basketball and lacrosse.[5]

In 1897 a Dartford diplomate, Miss Rhoda Anstey, opened at

Halesowen in Warwickshire another training college for women teachers of physical education. Miss Anstey followed Madame Bergman-Österberg's adaptation of the Ling system. Two other pioneers at first did not: Miss Dorette Wilke, who in 1898 started classes at the Chelsea Polytechnic, and the Misses Beatrice and Evelyn Bear, who had earlier opened a training school in London. But both establishments found it difficult to place their diplomates in posts, so both changed over to the Bergman-Österberg programme.

Music

From the earliest days the residential colleges trained students to teach singing. By the end of the nineteenth century many were also providing facilities for practising instrumental music. But none trained specialists. Until 1887, when the Tonic-Sol-Fa College instituted a School Teachers Music Certificate, there were no specialist qualifications available to training college students. A relatively small number of students began to take this Certificate; in 1894, for example, 105, from seven colleges. The Certificate was restricted to the teaching of singing.

Art

Drawing was included in the training college course at an early date. But the idea of teachers of *art* in Public Elementary schools did not exist. Drawing was important as a pre-vocational subject; art, as a means of creative expression or aesthetic enjoyment, had no place in schooling, and consequently none in teacher-training. The certificates awarded by the National Art Training School, established in 1837 and transferred in 1856 to the Education Department, were wholly unconcerned with the *teaching* of art. Similarly, the lower level qualifications offered by some provincial art schools contained no teaching element, despite such titles as 'The Art Master's Certificate' and 'The Art Class Teacher's Certificate'.

'Manual Instruction'

The training of teachers of 'manual instruction', that is, of woodwork and metalwork, was the only form of specialist training pioneered by a statutory body. The London School Board, egged on by the first director of the City and Guilds of London Institute (CGLI), Mr P (later Sir Philip) Magnus, mounted in 1887 an experiment in six schools of which the principal feature was the generous allowance of time that was allocated to manual instruction. The undoubted success of this experiment encouraged the School Board, the Institute, and several men's training colleges, to start regular courses for teachers of woodwork and metalwork. The courses attracted few students before 1892, when the CGLI introduced a Manual Training Teacher's Certificate in woodwork. It followed this in 1894 with a similar Certificate in metalwork. In 1898 a semi-official Board of Examinations for Educational Handwork was established jointly by the Education Department, the Educational Handwork Association, and the Associations of Headmasters and Headmistresses. The certificates awarded by this Board were recognised by the Education Department as approved qualifications for teachers of handwork in Public Elementary schools. But there were few takers. Teachers of manual instruction were not regarded by their classroom colleagues as members of staff, and woodwork and metalwork—taught in 'centres', away from the schools—were not considered authentic elements of the curriculum.

Special Educational Treatment

Special educational treatment for handicapped children did not become a statutory obligation until 1893, and then only in respect of blind and deaf children. But voluntary effort had begun doing the job twenty years earlier. In 1872 Mr F J (later Sir Francis) Campbell, an American blinded in childhood, with Mr T R Armitage, an Irishman whose sight was failing, founded at Norwood a Royal Normal College and Academy of music, designed to educate blind people and "qualify them to earn a living as organists, teachers, and pianoforte tuners".[6] Before long Norwood-trained teachers were being employed in Board schools, especially in London.

In 1886–89 a Royal Commission investigated the education and employment of blind, deaf, dumb, and mentally defective persons. Among its recommendations were: (1) teachers of the blind should be certificated teachers, and (2) the training colleges for teachers of the deaf should be put under Government supervision. The latter reflected the consequences of a long controversy about two systems of teaching deaf people: the 'Oral', designed to enable learners to speak, and the 'Sign and Manual', which did not. The controversy had led to the founding of rival associations, each of which had embarked on training teachers. As the Royal Commission's recommendation was not implemented, the two types of training went on. Not until 1915 were the warring associations induced to amalgamate.

References

1 *Minutes of the Committee of Council 1854–55,* p. 473.
2 The Merit grant was introduced as an incentive to better work. A grant of one shilling (5p), two shillings (10p), or three shillings (15p) per head was awarded to schools rated by HMI as 'Fair', 'Good', or 'Excellent'.
3 Miss Bergman was the second Superintendent of Physical Education for Girls appointed by the London School Board. The first, Miss Concordia Lofving, also a graduate of the Stockholm *Centralinstitutet,* was appointed in 1878, but left after little more than a year. The School Board was not at that time unanimously in favour of the experiment.
4 May, Jonathan, *Madame Bergman-Österberg,* Harrap, for the University of London Institute of Education, 1969, p. 33.
5 ibid., p. 74, and *ILEA 'Contact',* 16 May 1975, p. 23.
6 *The Times,* 10 May 1873. Quoted from Pritchard, D G, *Education and the Handicapped,* Routledge and Kegan Paul, 1963, p. 73.

CHAPTER EIGHT

In-Service Training

In-service training of teachers is older than initial training, but during the first half of the nineteenth century there was often no clear line of demarcation between the two. They could be, and frequently were, identical. The training of monitors and pupil-teachers—or at any rate of first-year pupil-teachers—was both initial and in-service.

The British and National Societies from an early date employed 'organising masters' to travel from place to place advising teachers on how to form and conduct Monitorial schools. Both Societies also arranged evening classes and lectures and, from the 1840s or before, 'summer schools' and 'harvest holiday camps' for teachers. Some of these vacation courses were in session for as long as six weeks, but probably most teachers attended for only a week or so.

Whether many of the classes and lectures were sufficiently rigorous to be called training is an open question. But one venture, the 'Singing School for Schoolmasters and Schoolmistresses' begun by John Pyke Hullah[1] in 1841, was a very serious enterprise. Open to all "persons engaged in elementary education, either in day schools, Sunday schools, or evening schools",[2] it offered a thorough training in the teaching of singing, and did much to establish this subject in Public Elementary schools.

During the 1830s and 1840s there was a revival of 'mutual improvement societies' among Elementary school teachers (these had been known in the eighteenth century). Professor Asher Tropp has told how London teachers in British schools asked their Society for money:

> to form an association, with the object of going through regular

courses of study, passing examinations, holding meetings, lectures and essay and discussion groups on the government and discipline of schools and the best methods of teaching.[3]

The Society agreed—not without misgivings—and in 1836 the 'British Teachers' Quarterly Association' began to hold meetings at Borough Road. Two years later National Society teachers similarly banded together.

During the 1850s the number of evening classes and summer schools seems to have decreased, probably because of the rapid growth of pupil-teaching and the subsequent increasing proportion of Certificated teachers in grant-aided Elementary schools. But this decade saw the beginning of what was to become one of the largest part-time enterprises for teachers during the nineteenth century; preparing for the examinations leading to the certificates offered to teachers by the Department of Science and Art. In 1859 the Department instituted an examination for teachers of science which became particularly popular in the bleak years following Robert Lowe's Revised Code, because the holder of a 'South Kensington' certificate[4] had the right to teach in evening school as well as day school, and could thus augment considerably his earnings.

In the 1850s Thomas Henry Huxley, then a young lecturer at the Government School of Mines and Science, began his lifelong struggle to get the importance of science recognised in schools and colleges. At the School of Mines, Certificated teachers and members of the College of Preceptors were admitted half-price to lectures; this gave Huxley the idea of building up the School into a national institution for training science teachers. Among the many means he employed towards this end the most effective was the series of summer schools for teachers which he started in 1871. So successful were these schools that by 1881 Huxley's ambition was achieved; the School of Mines was renamed the Normal School of Science, and he was made its Dean. But the venture was short-lived; when Huxley retired in 1885 the new title was dropped, and the training of teachers came to an end.

Until the last decade of the nineteenth century most in-service training of teachers comprised single lectures, or short series of lectures such as, for example, those given in 1873 and 1874 at the College of Preceptors by Professor Joseph Payne. The lectures were sometimes supplemented by group discussion. In 1890 an entirely new departure was made by the Education Department when it introduced into training colleges the one-year 'Supplementary' course, designed to enable teachers to complete a degree or acquire a specialist qualification. Supplementary courses were at first intended primarily for students who had just completed a Certificate course, but they were also made available to serving teachers. Unfortunately, the grants offered were so small that few teachers could afford to come.

References

1 John Pyke Hullah (1812–84), a friend of Kay-Shuttleworth, went at his request to Paris to study the 'fixed doh' method of teaching singing. This method he used at Battersea, and demonstrated all over the country; he made it so popular that it was adopted not only in Elementary but also in 'middle-class' and 'public' schools. Concerts which he gave in the years 1841–3 were attended by the Prince Consort, the Duke of Wellington, and many other people eminent in public life. He later became Professor of Music at King's College, London.
2 *Minutes of the Committee of Council 1840–41*, p. 27.
3 Tropp, Asher, *The School Teachers:* The Growth of the Teaching Profession in England and Wales from 1800 to the present day. Heinemann, 1957, p. 44.
4 So called because the Department of Science and Art was housed at South Kensington. The Education Department was in Whitehall.

CHAPTER NINE

"Exit the Pupil-Teacher"

The last decade of the nineteenth century was rich in promise of better things to come in English education. The first decade of the twentieth did much to redeem that promise. Many persons helped to shape the reforms then made, but amongst them one was pre-eminent: Robert Laurie Morant, Permanent Secretary to the Board of Education from 1903 to 1911.

"One of the objects on which he had throughout set his heart," wrote his biographer Mr Bernard Allen, "was the improvement of the quality of the teachers in elementary schools."[1] Morant's greatest achievement will no doubt always be reckoned his swift build-up of a statutory system of secondary education; but the changes he made in the education and training of teachers were of fundamental importance; and it is essential to realise how closely linked the two reforms were. One of Morant's main reasons for developing secondary education was to secure better teachers for Public Elementary schools.

All nineteenth century experience had shown that the first, and absolutely necessary, prerequisite for securing better teachers was an improvement in their general education. To effect that in 1900 meant improving the general education of pupil-teachers, for they consti-tuted virtually the sole source of recruitment to Elementary school teaching, and in addition made up nearly one-quarter of the teaching force (30,783 out of 139,818) in the schools. (No wonder the 1898 Departmental Committee judged the pupil-teacher system too firmly embedded in the national economy of education to be abolished or radically altered!)

In the schools in 1900 there was also a relatively small number of 'probationers'. These were boys and girls, of any age from thirteen to sixteen, who were not, like pupil-teachers, committed to teaching as a profession—though actually most of them did become teachers. No paper qualifications were necessary to become a probationer, but only evidence of good health and sound character. Probationers who wished to become pupil-teachers had, however, to pass before they attained the age of sixteen an examination set by the Board of Education, or one giving exemption from it. Probationers were allowed to teach up to one-half of the school week.

When the Board of Education took over from the Committee of Council on 1 April 1900 the minimum age at which boys and girls could become pupil-teachers was fourteen; but from 1 July it was to be fifteen, except in cases authorised by HMI—which meant in effect that exceptions could be made in rural areas.

To qualify for acceptance as a pupil-teacher an applicant had to:

1 Be approved by HMI.

2 Pass an examination, set by the Board of Education, in Reading and Recitation, English, History, Geography, Arithmetic, Algebra. Euclid (boys) or Needlework (girls), and Teaching.

3 Pass a medical examination.

For applicants seeking to serve in Church schools there was also stringent enquiry into both their own moral state and that of their homes.

The number of pupil-teachers permitted to a school depended on the number of Certificated teachers; in 1900 it might not exceed three for the head teacher and one each for other Certificated teachers. This included probationers.

Pupil-teachers were not allowed to teach for more than five hours in any one day, or more than twenty in a week. Or so said the Code. But to appreciate the situation in 1900 one must realise that what happened in schools was sometimes very different from what was laid down by the Code. In the areas of enlightened School Boards practice could be better than the rule; London, for example, limited its pupil-teachers to three hours' teaching a day, the minimum allowed by the Code. But cases like the following, recorded by a woman who became a pupil-teacher about 1900, were probably not uncommon, especially in rural areas.

> I started in school when I was 9½ years old. The school was short of teachers, so a girl had to be borrowed from the upper department to look after the babies. As grants were paid by results and the top classes couldn't possibly be spared, the master said to me: "See what you can do" ... By the time I was thirteen I had a class of 40 infants.[2]

When this highly experienced young woman applied for recognition as a pupil-teacher she failed the qualifying examination in—of all things!—teaching. This was not so surprising, though, as might seem; as she confessed, she had "just mimicked ... the Infants' mistress". Happily, someone had the sense to send the girl to another school, where ultimately she gained a King's Scholarship.

Pupil-teachers were examined annually by HMI. Failure could mean termination of their contract. On completing their term of service they could sit the Queen's (from 1901, King's) Scholarship examination. A first or second class pass in this qualified the holder for entry into training college—but could not guarantee it, because applicants were far more numerous than places. In 1900 barely 44.5 per cent of qualified pupil-teachers got in.

A pupil-teacher's chance of entering college varied greatly, for two main reasons: (1) his religious denomination, and (2) the availability (and quality) of a Pupil-Teacher Centre. Members of the Church of England had a built-in advantage, because they had sole access to 30 out of the 55 training colleges. Pupil-teachers in the areas of well-to-do and progressive School Boards had a great advantage, because these provided excellent Pupil-Teacher Centres. Small School Boards, and most Voluntary schools, could offer at best evening and/or Saturday classes. No wonder the streamlined urban Centres practically monopolised the top end of the Scholarship list.

A pupil-teacher who failed to get into training college had four options: (1) try to get a place the following year; with a good testimonial from HMI, this was possible; (2) take a teaching post, and study in spare time for the Acting Teacher's Certificate; (3) resign himself to a career as an uncertificated teacher, on a lower salary than a Certificated teacher—not too bad if one liked a quiet country life; (4) seek fortune in some other occupation.

Before the 1902 Education Act came into operation the Board had little power to improve the pupil-teacher/training college situation. The Act completely altered the position, a fact of which Morant quickly took advantage. In July 1903 he issued *Regulations for the Instruction and Training of Pupil-Teachers and Students in Training Colleges.* These, the first such Regulations to be issued in a separate volume, contained what amounted in total to revolutionary change. Those affecting training colleges will be outlined in Chapter 10; those affecting pupil-teachers were as follows:

1 From 1 August 1904 the minimum age for recognition as a pupil-teacher would be raised from fifteen to sixteen, "except in a few rural districts".

2 From 1 August 1904 probationers would not be recognised as members of the staff of a school.

3 From 1 August 1905 no pupil-teacher might teach for more than half the school week.

4 From 1 August 1905 all pupil-teachers must receive "approved courses of instruction", amounting to at least 300 hours a year, and given, "wherever possible", in "fully equipped and staffed Pupil-Teacher Centres" approved by the Board of Education.

5 From 1 August 1905 pupil-teachers were to be employed only in "schools specially selected for the purpose".

LEAs could, if they wished, anticipate these dates; a number did.

To gain the Board's approval a Pupil-Teacher Centre had to be open for five meetings a week of not less than two hours each, in not fewer than 36 weeks a year. The curriculum had to include:

Reading and Recitation   Voice Production   Drawing   Music
Natural Science   Physical Exercises   Needlework (girls)

"A Higher Elementary School or a suitable Secondary School" would be a desirable place for the instruction of boys and girls intending to be pupil-teachers; but as in many districts neither would be available, the Regulations provided for the establishment of "full-time Preparatory Classes" at Pupil-Teacher Centres for pupils under the age of sixteen.

These epoch-making Regulations were intended, said Morant in a Prefatory Memorandum, to facilitate:

1 The deferral of employment as a Pupil-Teacher in an Elementary school, so as to allow more time for a prospective teacher's general education.

2 The continuation of that general education under reasonable circumstances during the period of apprenticeship as a Pupil-Teacher.

Morant urged that wherever possible boys and girls intending to become pupil-teachers should spend three or four years in a Secondary school. To this end he asked LEAs to arrange:

> by means of an adequate scholarship system or otherwise, that all the cleverest candidates for Pupil-Teacherships ... should receive a sound general education in a Secondary School for three or four years, with schoolfellows intended for other careers, before they commence service in any capacity in an Elementary School.

Reactions to the Regulations were mixed. Dr T J Macnamara, MP, a former NUT vice-president, thought them "the most admirable educational monograph he had ever read".[3] But some LEAs feared that the raising of the age of entry into apprenticeship would diminish the supply of pupil-teachers—and how right they-were!—because working-class parents could not afford the loss of wages. The response to Morant's appeal for scholarships was similarly various. London, for example, increased the number of its 'Junior County' scholarships. So did Somerset. But Northumberland, and other LEAs, felt that the Regulations imposed "an unduly heavy burden on the local rates".

Though the NUT's official attitude resembled Dr Macnamara's, many members of the Union rejected the principle that a pupil-teacher's service in an Elementary school should be regarded as "a time of probation and training rather than of too early practice in teaching". Their belief in the value of early practice was not always entirely disinterested; without pupil-teachers, many Elementary schools would have had to close. In 1900 there was only one Certificated teacher to 75 pupils, only one *trained* teacher to 128.

Whatever Morant's ambitions, there was in 1903 no possibility that all, or even most, prospective teachers could get three or four years in a recognised Secondary school. There were not enough schools, and those in existence were unevenly distributed. So, while building up a national network of Secondary schools, he made it also his business to expand and improve the Pupil-Teacher Centres.

These varied greatly in character and quality. In a few places—notably Scarborough—boys and girls could attend a Centre attached to the Secondary school in which they had received their general education. At Bristol the Centres, while not housed in Secondary schools, were in effect affiliated to them. At Leeds, on the other hand, both the Municipal and the Roman Catholic Centres accepted applicants from any Secondary school in the district. A few Centres were attached to Technical colleges, and three, at Nottingham, Reading, and Southampton, to University colleges.

Centres ranged in size from 35–40 students to 800. Half-time attendance was widespread, but elsewhere students might attend for as little as three half-days a fortnight. Holidays varied from six to twelve weeks a year. At many Centres no fees were charged; at others students paid up to £5 a year. In general, the Centres provided by the large urban School Boards were the best housed, staffed, and equipped; with rare exceptions, such as the Roman Catholic Centre at Leeds, the Voluntary bodies could not compete with them.

The quality of the education they gave also varied, but suffered from one common defect. The 1898 Committee had commented shrewdly on this.

> The best of [the Centres] are provided with all the necessary apparatus and staff for excellent secondary training, which the conditions of their existence prevent them from giving ... It is inevitable that they should tend to produce professional and social narrowness of aim, and to subordinate educational aims to pressure of examinations.[4]

Morant warned them in 1903 that the Board of Education intended to supervise more closely than previously their organisation and curriculum. In 1905 he listed the subjects they must include, and told them the amounts of time they must spend on the more important. The subjects were:

English language, literature and composition;

Reading and Recitation, including voice production;
A language other than English;
History, Geography; Music where possible;
Elementary Mathematics, including Arithmetic;
Elementary Science, including practical work;
Drawing, Physical exercises, Manual work (boys), Needlework (girls).

Not less than half the time was to be spent on English, History, Geography, and languages. Wherever possible, some or all of the students should study a foreign language; with the Board's approval they could study two. If a Centre was attached to a Secondary school or a Higher Elementary school its studies were to be co-ordinated with those of the school.[5]

In the same Regulations the Board of Education announced the abolition, after 1906, of King's Scholarships.[6] The reasons given for the ending of this longstanding award—an integral part of the original Pupil-Teacher scheme of 1846—were that:

1 The Government grant which a student earned by winning a King's Scholarship was no longer a grant to an individual student, but "a grant towards the maintenance of Training Colleges".

2 Entry into training college was no longer restricted to students who passed 'creditably' in the King's Scholarship examination; it could be, and increasingly was, secured by passing other examinations.

3 Many King's Scholars did not enter college, but went straight into teaching posts.

In place of the King's Scholarship examination there would be from 1907 a 'Preliminary Examination for the Elementary School Teachers Certificate'. This would be different from the King's Scholarship examination in two important respects. Part I, which as in the previous examination would cover the basic Elementary school subjects, would be a qualifying examination. It would be held in December, and only those students who passed would be allowed to sit Part II, held the following April. Secondly, there would be no classified honours list; successful candidates would all be placed alphabetically in a single list. In some subjects, however, the mark of Distinction might be awarded.

The whole of Part I would be compulsory. Part II, which covered students' personal education, would contain a compulsory core consisting of the three subjects English, History, and Geography. Candidates would also have to sit three, or more, optional subjects selected from three groups: Elementary Mathematics, Elementary Science, and Foreign Languages. At least one subject must be chosen from each group.

The curricular changes seem to have been generally welcomed. The abolition of the honours list was highly unpopular, and not only with students; staff feared that it would lead to a lowering of standards.

These changes were the prelude to larger ones. In April 1907 Morant issued Regulations "for the Preliminary Education of Elementary School Teachers".[7] The omission from the title of any mention of pupil-teachers was deliberate; the principal purpose of the Regulations was to introduce "an alternative to the traditional method of Pupil-Teachership" for entry into training college. From August 1907 selected pupils at Secondary schools could be awarded 'Bursaries', that is, grants to enable them to stay an additional year at school between the ages of sixteen and eighteen. On completing this year they could enter training college straight away, or alternatively could serve in schools as 'Student Teachers' for up to one year and then enter college.

No examination qualification would be required for recognition as a Bursar, but from August 1909 the Board of Education would recognise only applicants who had been pupils at a recognised Secondary school for at least the three previous years, and would pay grant only on Bursars who passed, either during their Bursary year or within one year thereafter, one of the examinations qualifying for entry into training college. So that those who qualified at an early age might enter training college without delay, Bursars would be accepted at seventeen, a year earlier than pupil-teachers.

Morant was doubtless encouraged to introduce this scheme by the report (published later in the year) of a committee of HMIs which queried

whether [the pupil-teacher system] is worth keeping in existence at all, whether the continuous contact with the child mind ... is worth struggling for at the cost of the disorganisation of the Secondary schools and the overwork, dissipation of energies, and in many cases neglect, which are too often the result of the half-time system to the pupil-teachers themselves.[8]

LEAs on the whole liked the Bursary scheme—in its Student-Teacher form. Many teachers did not; in fact, it brought to a head a storm that had been rumbling for years.

The Schoolmaster, official journal of the NUT, published a summary of the Regulations under the ominous title of "Exit the Pupil-Teacher", and asserted that "The old-style pupil-teacher will soon be as extinct as the dodo".[9] Nevertheless, the paper apparently welcomed the new scheme, as "a tremendous step ... in advance", and had "no fear that the average of teaching skills is going to be lowered; provided that the training colleges rise to the task".[10] But many teachers were full of fear, being convinced that standards must fall. As the president of the National Federation of Class Teachers said succinctly: "The new type of training may foster students, but it cannot create teachers."[11]

The Bursary scheme was also criticised widely as being unfair to working-class parents, because it meant serious postponement of their children's wage-earning. In the days before either national health or unemployment insurance, many parents could simply not afford to forego a child's earnings until the age of twenty or twenty-one. Some critics even alleged that there was deliberate discrimination, that the scheme was:

> a case of the upper classes trying to 'down' the working man ... under the Bursary system the working man could not possibly put any of his children into the teaching profession.[12]

There was reason for the belief that the Bursary scheme must inevitably accelerate sharply the already persistent decline in the number of young recruits to the teaching profession. In 1906–7 the number of pupil-teachers newly recognised was 11,018; by 1913–14 it had fallen to 1,691. And this number was supplemented by only 3,012 new bursars.

As early as 1909 the President of the Board of Education, Mr

Walter Runciman, declared that the pupil-teacher system was "dying out all over the country".[13] This was true; though the recruitment of pupil-teachers lingered on here and there up to the outbreak of the Second World War, it was pretty well extinct by the outbreak of the First.

References

1   Allen, Bernard, *Sir Robert Morant: A Great Public Servant*, Macmillan, 1934, p. 208.
2   Miss Annie Gaukrodger, in a letter dated 2 June 1958 to Miss M A B Jones, then principal of S Katherine's College, Liverpool.
3   *Education*, 16 July 1903, p. 87.
4   *Report of the Departmental Committee on the Pupil-Teacher System*, 1898, p. 7.
5   *Regulations for the Instruction and Training of Pupil-Teachers 1905*, Article 13. (a).
6   ibid., Article 13 (b).
7   Cmd. 3444, dated 15 April 1907.
8   *General Report on the Instruction and Training of Pupil-Teachers 1903–07*, (Cmd. 3587), 1907, p. 25.
9   *The Schoolmaster*, 27 April 1907, p. 828. This was not, however, the first time the paper had made this doleful prophecy. See the issue of 14 July 1906.
10 ibid.
11 *The Schoolmaster*, 3 October 1908, p. 530.
12 *The Schoolmaster*, 18 April 1908. Report from Chelmsford.
13 *The Schoolmaster*, 25 May 1909. In a speech at the opening of Bingley Training College.

CHAPTER TEN

"A New Type of Training College"

Between 1890 and 1900 the residential training colleges, spurred on by the competition of the day training colleges, greatly enlarged and improved their facilities and amenities. They increased the number of their places from under 3,300 to over 4,000, provided many students' common rooms (rare before 1890), and improved libraries, laboratories, studios, and workshops. For all this they had to raise money privately; they had had no grants for capital expenditure since 1860.

But the total number of places in the colleges (day and residential) was still far from meeting either the demand from applicants or the needs of the schools. In January 1900 the residential colleges admitted 2,732 new entrants; but at the Queen's Scholarship examination held the previous month over 6,000 candidates had qualified for entry. The day training colleges took about 1,000 of these; that still left nearly half of the qualified candidates without a place. Such a shortfall had been endemic for many years. It was reflected in the make-up of the teaching force in the Elementary schools. In 1900 only just over one-quarter of the teachers (36,000 of 140,000) were college-trained.

"Voluntary effort," concluded Mr Scott Coward, Chief Inspector for Training Colleges, "is no longer equal to the task of overtaking this vast demand."[1] The Education Act 1902 implicitly acknowledged this by making clear, in Section 22, that the powers granted to LEAs to "supply or aid the supply of education other than elementary" included power to provide and maintain training colleges. In July 1903, only three months after the Act came into operation, the Board of Education issued Regulations for the training of teachers in which the LEAs were invited to help increase the number of training college places by subsidy to existing colleges, or by themselves providing colleges and/or hostels.

The Board's 1904 Regulations contained the historic announcement that:

> A new type of training college may be recognised which, though not in connection with a University or University College, need not on that account be a Residential College, as has hitherto been the case.[2]

In other words, LEAs could provide whatever kinds of colleges they wished.

The London County Council (LCC) had, thanks to promptings from Sir John Gorst, last Vice-President of the Committee of Council, long anticipated this announcement. In 1900 he suggested to County Councils that they had the necessary powers to undertake the training of teachers. The chairman of the Technical Education Board of the LCC, Mr Sidney Webb, took up the suggestion, and proposed that the Council should establish a day training college. The LCC would accept full financial responsibility, but to comply with the Board of Education's Regulations, which like those of the Committee of Council previously required day training colleges to be associated with a university institution, would invite London University to share the academic and administrative responsibility. The University agreed, and in 1902 'The University County Council Training College for London' was born.

It was unique. It was the first training college to be jointly administered by a university and a local authority. It trained teachers for all types of schools. It trained both post-graduate and under-graduate students. (The latter took a three-year course leading to both a degree and a teacher's diploma.) Its principal was also the professor of education in the university.

Mr Adam Rankine, HMI, hailed it as:

> the connecting link between the old and the new ... the fulfilment of those ideas with regard to the higher education and the longer training of the teacher, and the bringing of elementary into vital union with secondary education which created the University Day Training Colleges and transformed the Residential.[3]

Alas! Mr Rankine was too optimistic. When the four-year course leading to a degree and a post-graduate Teacher's Certificate was introduced in 1911 the college was restricted to post-graduate training.

In 1904 the LCC acquired another training college. In 1898 the London School Board had established a training centre designed to assist three types of serving teachers: (1) ex-pupil-teachers who had failed to get into training college or could not go because they could not leave home; (2) untrained teachers employed part-time; and (3) older uncertificated teachers who wished to get the Acting Teacher's Certificate. The LSB had provided two- and three-year courses, and had recognised, and paid, as Certificated teachers all students who successfully completed their course, despite the fact that the Board of Education refused them recognition. As the centre had done extremely good work, the LCC asked the Board to recognise it as a training college. The Board agreed, but restricted it to women.

In 1905 London University became solely responsible for a training institution. The Goldsmiths' Company, one of the wealthiest of the City of London Livery Companies, had since 1891 maintained a large Technical and Recreational Institute at New Cross in south-east London. With the passing of the Education Act 1902, and the consequential Education (London) Act 1903, the Company felt that public education should become increasingly the function of public authorities. In 1904 it proposed to hand over the Institute not, as might perhaps have been expected, to the LCC, but to London University. The sole condition it made was that the property must always be used for educational purposes; it added the suggestion that:

> because of the great need for well-qualified teachers, after the 1902 Education Act, the existing buildings at New Cross might serve the purpose of a University College for South London, "to which the teachers from any part of the Metropolis might be drafted".[4]

London University accepted the gift, though it presented a formidable financial problem. The Goldsmiths' had promised grants of £5,000 a year for five years, but the annual cost of maintenance was about £15,000. In these circumstances a teacher-training department could be a gold mine, provided that a regular and sufficiently large supply of students could be ensured, and that the

Board of Education would recognise the college for grant. The University secured the necessary guarantees from the Board, the LCC, and the LEAs in the Home Counties, and in September 1905 "The University of London Goldsmiths' College" was opened. It comprised an art school, a technical department, and a teacher training department of 500 students.

Outside London, LEAs did not respond enthusiastically to the Government's invitation to establish training colleges, for two main reasons: (1) the cost, especially of maintenance, for which no special grants were offered, and (2) their fear of 'poaching', that is, that LEAs which did not provide colleges would 'steal' teachers trained by their neighbours who did. To overcome these difficulties various schemes for joint provision of colleges were mooted, but none came to fruition. Another solution, widely advocated, was that teacher training should be a central, not a local, function. In 1904, for example, the first president of the Association of Education Committees (AEC), Mr J Tudor Walters, in his presidential address called for "a national system of training colleges", adding, interestingly, "by preference affiliated with the universities".[5]

Neither the Conservative government then in power, nor the Liberal government which succeeded it in 1905, favoured this policy. But in 1906 the Liberals offered a substantially improved rate of grant: up to "75 per cent in respect of all capital expenditure incurred by them (the LEAs) for the provision of sites and buildings for Training Colleges".[6] Even this did not greatly stimulate LEA effort, partly because nothing was offered for maintenance, and partly because of the fear of 'poaching'.

The first LEA to open a training college under the 1904 Regulations was Herefordshire. It was a fully residential college, for 100 women. The next was Sheffield, in 1905. In 1906 London opened Avery Hill, in 1907 Bolton, Leeds, and Portsmouth established colleges. But by the outbreak of war in 1914 there were only twenty LEA colleges; hardly an impressive achievement for 146 local authorities for higher education in an immensely rich country.

The 1904 Regulations had specifically stated that the "new type of training College" need not be residential. But Herefordshire, Leeds, and London all established residential colleges; and by 1914 all the other LEA colleges were providing hostels, mainly for women, this having been made a condition of grant. Gradually the distinction between a 'residential' college—in which both living and teaching accommodation were in one building or block of buildings—and one providing residence in detached 'hostels' was to become increasingly blurred. What did persist was the belief that residence was an essential element in the training of an Elementary school teacher.

Most of the training colleges founded between 1904 and 1914 were administratively of conventional pattern. Sheffield was an exception. The day training college associated with the University College had been severely criticised by HMI, and a final blow came in 1903, when the Board of Education informed the University College that if its application for a University Charter succeeded, the Board would not recognise its training college as part of the University. At about the same time, however, the University College learned that the City Council was considering establishing a training college. So it offered to close the day training college, to transfer its students to the City college, and, to give the latter a good start, to recruit a larger than normal intake in September 1904.

The City college, which opened in October 1905, nevertheless quickly ran into trouble. The Board of Education refused to recognise for grant the transferred students, who were doing a three-year course leading to a degree and the Teacher's Certificate, unless the work of the University and the Training College was more closely co-ordinated. To do this an elaborate agreement was arranged. The academic work of all the Training College students was to be directed by a joint Board of Studies. Students who had matriculated before entering the college were required to do a three-year course. The principal of the Training College was made a member of the University Senate. The Teacher's Certificates were to be signed both by him and the University Vice-Chancellor. And the training college was renamed 'The University of Sheffield Teachers College'. This cumbrous arrangement, which chafed everybody, mercifully lasted only three years; in 1908 the College became a normal two-year training institution. Happily, co-operation between University and College lasted much longer.

Competition from LEA colleges embarrassed some denominational colleges to the extent that by 1906 they could not fill all their places, although overall demand was still greater than the supply. The main difficulty was their insistence on accepting only candidates of their own denomination. In 1907 a ham-handed attempt was made by the

President of the Board of Education, Mr Reginald McKenna, to solve this problem. In July he issued Regulations which included the following provisions:

1 In and after 1908 the application of a candidate [to a training college] may in no circumstances be rejected on the ground of religious faith, or by reason of his refusal to undertake to attend or abstain from attending any place of religious worship, or any religious observance, or instruction in religious subjects in the Colleges or elsewhere; nor on the ground of social antecedents or the like.

2 After 1 August 1907 no institution not already recognised as a Training College (or Hostel) will be so recognised unless it complies with Sections 7 (g) and 7 (h).[7]

These two sub-sections laid down that:

1 No member of the teaching staff is to be required to belong to a particular denomination.

2 No majority on a Governing Body is to belong, or not to belong, to a particular denomination.

3 No denominational religious instruction is to be taught in College or Hostel except on a written request from the parent, and then out of private funds.

In short, these Regulations meant the end of denominational colleges as such. They were designed to ensure that all grant-aided training colleges would be "open to all candidates who are qualified to profit by a course of training, irrespective of religious convictions or social status".[8] The Board of Education warned colleges whose trust deeds forbade obedience to the Regulations that:

It would be for Authorities of the College to decide whether ... they are desirous of continuing to receive grants from public funds, and in that event to obtain an amendment of their trusts if needed.[9]

From the Anglicans and the Roman Catholics came violent protest, from Nonconformists paeans of rejoicing. On 20 July the Archbishop of Canterbury led an imposing delegation to the Prime Minister, Sir

Henry Campbell Bannerman, but received only a dusty answer from the President of the Board of Education. Five days later an even more impressive delegation arrived, led by Archbishop Bourne, head of the Roman Catholic hierarchy in Great Britain, and including England's premier peer, the Duke of Norfolk. This delegation had a much more satisfying (though not more satisfactory) interview, perhaps because its members were more pugnacious than the Protestants, who seem to have put their case rather diffidently. The Roman Catholics told the Prime Minister bluntly that:

> There are some of these new Regulations that we cannot possibly accept, and ... shall certainly disregard.[10]

The Duke of Norfolk repeated the defiance on the same day in the House of Lords. But the Board of Education would not budge an inch. It was doubtless greatly encouraged by the unanimous and cordial support of the Free Churches, who also came in deputation—to express deep gratitude for the Regulations.

While the leaders of the Churches lobbied the Government their supporters conducted a violent controversy in the Press. But gradually the necessity for a compromise became evident. The LCC Education Committee emphasised this early in 1908; it asked the Board of Education to modify the Regulations, not for denominational reasons, but simply to prevent the closure of the Church of England training colleges in its area.

By July 1908 a compromise was agreed between the Archbishop of Canterbury and a new President of the Board of Education, Mr Walter Runciman. In the year 1908–9 no denominational college would be compelled to accept more than one-half of its applicants without reference to their religious affiliation. The agreement was for one year only. It worked, and was never rescinded.

On this issue the Board of Education was defeated. But that did not deflect it from a policy of strengthening its grip on the administration of the training colleges. By 1908 it had made its approval obligatory for the founding of a new college or the enlargement of an existing one, for all appointments to the academic staff; for the number of students a college might admit, and the entry qualifications to be required; for the length of courses, and for the introduction of new courses or the substantial alteration of existing ones.

In 1907 the Board of Education at long last recognised the

Domestic Subjects colleges for grant at teacher-training rates. But its Regulations[11] imposed conditions which some of them could not meet. By 1914 only fourteen had secured recognition; significantly, nine of these were LEA colleges. The specialist colleges of physical education did not seek recognition. By 1914 there were five, including the department at the Chelsea Polytechnic. To the three nineteenth century foundations had been added in 1900 one at Liverpool, established by Miss Irene M Marsh, and in 1903 one at Bedford, established by Miss Margaret Stansfeld, who had been one of Madame Bergman-Österberg's assistants at Hampstead.

During the first dozen years of the twentieth century a quiet revolution began to take place in the day training colleges. By 1914 over half of them had acquired secondary training departments. Not very large departments, it is true, because of the reluctance of men to undergo training, and also, one suspects, because, as the Board of Education confessed in its last Report before the war, "the existing kind of training has not the confidence of some of the persons who ought to be best qualified to form an opinion upon it".[12] But secondary departments had come to stay, and, like the baby cuckoos, to push the other inhabitants out of the nest. The introduction of the four-year course was ultimately to transform the day training colleges into university departments devoted almost exclusively to training teachers for Secondary schools.

References

1 *General Reports of HM Inspectors on Elementary Schools and Training Colleges for the year 1901*, p. 174.
2 *Regulations for the Training of Teachers and for the Examination of Students in Training Colleges 1904*, Article 2 (a).
3 *General Reports of HM Inspectors on Elementary Schools and Training Colleges for the year 1902*, p. 172.
4 Dymond, Dorothy (ed.), *The Forge:* The History of Goldsmiths' College 1905–1955, Methuen, 1955, p. 4.
5 *Education*, 13 October 1904, p. 283.
6 *Regulations for the Training of Teachers and for the Examination of Students in Training Colleges 1906*, Article 64.
7 *Regulations for the Training of Teachers and for the Examination of Students in Training Colleges 1907*, Section 8 (d).
8 *Report of the Board of Education 1906–1907*, p. 17.

9 ibid., p. 57.

10 *The Schoolmaster,* 3 August 1907, p. 217.

11 *Regulations for the Training of Teachers of Domestic Subjects 1907.* These were issued on 17 September 1907.

12 *Report of the Board of Education 1912–1913, p. 178.*

CHAPTER ELEVEN

Academic or Professional?

The purpose for which a Training College is recognised and aided by the Board of Education is the training of teachers for service in Public Elementary Schools.

That sentence, from Morant's Prefatory Memorandum to the 1904 Regulations for the training of teachers, looks at first sight like a blinding glimpse into the obvious. Actually, it was an aggressive statement of policy. The cause of it was spelled out clearly in the Board's Report for 1904–5.

> It is only gradually that the true function of Training Colleges can be differentiated from the multiplicity of educational duties which circumstances have hitherto cast upon them; nor is it desirable that they should ever cease to be places of study. But if the students are to get the benefit of the professional training which is the first reason for their being there at all, it is essential that their chief energies should not be given to some branch of special study not justified either by their strength or their ability.[1]

There was a long story behind the Board's statement. The central issue was whether training college students should, in any number, read for a university degree while doing a Teacher's Certificate course. Morant felt that many students, often with the connivance of their teachers, tended to neglect their Certificate work and give their main attention to their degree studies. Ironically, a recent reform effected by the Board had made this easier to do. From 1902 it had discontinued its examination of Part I (i.e. the professional subjects) at the end of the students' first year, and introduced a two-year continuous course, with periodical inspections, but no examination before the end.[2] This clearly offered a golden opportunity for students who opted for a university course in place of Part 2 to concentrate from the start on degree studies, trusting that a hasty cram towards the end of their second year would get them through Part I. It meant taking a considerable risk, for the two-year course was a formidable one. The committee which devised it thought it would be:

> exceedingly difficult and often impossible to find time for anything beyond the necessary professional training and instruction in general subjects which is essential to the proper equipment of all teachers.[3]

The committee had advised against two-year students taking university courses. It recommended the provision of more three-year courses, though aware that even some three-year students undertook degree studies "to the detriment of their purely professional training".

> In order to counteract the undue extension of this practice, we have endeavoured, in drawing up our courses to accentuate the necessity for every student to keep in view the professional, as distinguished from the academic side of his studies.[4]

The committee's warning about the danger of concurrent study for degree and Certificate was but the latest of many such warnings. In 1899 (to go no further back) Mr Scott Coward had commented that:

> The student, ardent and ambitious of the distinction of a degree, is unhappily often ill-prepared to undertake with any facility the university course; and after a severe ordeal of study, much of which is devoid of any power to stimulate the intellect ... he leaves with a degree ... but with very little of what a degree is supposed to betoken. Nor does he leave a better teacher.[5]

In 1901 Mr Coward said roundly: "I deprecate the attempt to force large numbers of our King's Scholars through university curricula for which they are not fit."[6] Examination results justified his words. In 1900, of second-year men who took a university course instead of Part 2, 70 per cent failed. The women were not so bad, but even their failure rate was nearly 50 per cent.

In December 1902 the Board of Education took drastic action. It announced that from 1904 onwards:

> students in residential colleges who substitute a university examination for part of their Certificate examination and fail in this examination will only be able to become Certificated teachers by passing the Acting Teacher's examination.[7]

In other words, they would leave college as uncertificated teachers. The NUT and the Associations of Training College Principals and Lecturers protested that the ruling seemed designed to deter residential college students from taking degree courses, and to discriminate against them, since it did not apply to students in day training colleges. But the Board did not give way; rather, it intensified its onslaught. In his Prefatory Memorandum to the 1904 Regulations Morant emphasised that:

> no college should aim at obtaining academical distinctions for its students if that involves either the over-straining of the powers of the student, or the neglect of his professional training.[8]

In 1905 he took even more drastic action; he announced in July, in Circular 530, that no student who entered a training college in or after 1907 would be allowed to take a course leading to a degree unless he had:

either

> passed the Preliminary Examination for the Certificate with distinction in English, History, and Geography; and in four optional subjects, including two languages;

or

> passed some other examination which the Board may feel able to accept as an equivalent thereto.[9]

Even with such qualifications, students would have to take in college courses in English, History, Geography, Elementary Mathematics and Science, unless they could produce evidence of having been adequately instructed in these subjects before entry. These conditions, as the Board's Report for 1904–5 acknowledged, were intended to ensure that:

> only those students whose general knowledge is wide and sure

enough and whose health is strong enough, shall prepare for university degrees.[10]

A year later Morant spoke still more strongly. In an open letter to the principal of King's College, London, the Revd A C Headlam, who had publicly protested against the 1905 Regulations, he said (in effect) that many training college students were, on entry into college, unfit to undertake university studies, and would be much better advised to content themselves with a less ambitious programme. Many teachers agreed with Morant. As *The Schoolmaster* said in July 1905:

> during the last fifteen years there has been an abuse of University work. Attracted by the bait of a degree, numbers of students of greater ambition than intellectual power have worked and strained and suffered, in a vain, or only partly successful, attempt to gain the magic letters.[11]

But substantial bodies of opinion in schools and training colleges were determined to fight Morant. Much more was involved, they declared, than the right of students to take university courses; what was at stake was the principle of academic freedom. That they raised this issue was both surprising and significant. Neither the schools nor the training colleges had ever had much academic—or any other—freedom. But in the Elementary School teachers' long and arduous struggle for status the university degree had become a symbol of prime importance. As nothing else, it offered proof that Elementary School teaching was not only a profession; it was a *learned* profession. Armed with this argument, and supported by statistics which showed that Borough Road and other colleges had for years been successfully undertaking concurrent study for Certificate and degree, they hardened their attitude. But so did Morant. In 1909 he laid down that from 1 August 1910 no examination certificate would qualify a student for entry into a degree course unless it showed that he had passed in:

> English Language and Literature, English History, Geography. A language selected from Latin, Greek, French, and German. Mathematics, and *either* a second language *or* an approved science.

Moreover, the candidate must have reached a higher standard than a bare pass in English Language and Literature and English History.[12]

Concurrently, however, Morant made the important suggestion that:

> the time is coming when all candidates who wish to take a degree course, and who have satisfied the conditions laid down by the Board to test their fitness for this work, should be admitted for a period of training of not less than three years, with a view to their completing a full degree course before they begin to teach.[13]

The universities thought three years not enough, and their view prevailed. In July 1911 the Board of Education made the historic announcement that it would recognise training departments attached to universities or university colleges as establishments providing a four-year course. The first three years would be devoted wholly or mainly to study for a degree, and the fourth to professional training for teaching in Public Elementary schools. To students who signed an undertaking to teach in maintained schools for a specified number of years after having qualified, the Board would make grants covering the tuition fees and maintenance throughout the four years.[14] This arrangement, which became known as 'The Pledge', was to persist for forty years, despite increasing distaste for it.

The wisdom, or otherwise, of concurrent Certificate and degree courses was only one facet—albeit the outstanding one—of a larger dispute: the correct balance to maintain between academic study and professional training in the preparation of Elementary school teachers. For many years there had been a tendency in the training colleges to overload the academic side. It was this tendency that Morant and his colleagues at the Board were determined to eliminate. That the four-year course which was a product of their campaign led ultimately to the separation of secondary from elementary training was an unhappy consequence of an essentially sound strategy.

References

1 *Report of the Board of Education 1904–5*, p. 40.
2 Circular 454, "A Two Years' Continuous Course of Study", dated 19 June

1901. The course was drawn up by a Departmental Committee under the chairmanship of Mr Henry Hobhouse, MP. It was incorporated in the *Day School Code of Regulations 1901* as Article 55.

3 *Report of the Board of Education 1900–01*, p. 539.
4 ibid., p. 538.
5 *Report of the Committee of Council 1898–99*, p. 322.
6 *General Reports of HM Inspectors on Elementary Schools and Training Colleges for the year 1901*, p. 179.
7 Circular 469, dated 15 December 1902.
8 *Regulations for the Training of Teachers and for the Examination of Students in Training Colleges 1904*, p. vii.
9 *Report of the Board of Education 1904–05*, p. 38.
10 ibid., p. 40.
11 *The Schoolmaster*, 1 July 1905, p. 19.
12 *Report of the Board of Education 1909–10*, p. 107.
13 ibid., p. 111.
14 *Statement of the Grants available from the Board of Education in aid of technological and professional work in Universities in England and Wales*. See Section 14 in *Board of Education Report on Universities and University Colleges 1909–10*, and Morant's Prefatory Memorandum to the *Regulations for the Training of Teachers for Elementary Schools 1911*.

CHAPTER TWELVE

Subject Specialists

The rapid growth of the statutory system of secondary education compelled the Board of Education to take action about the training of teachers for Secondary schools. In 1906 it gave notice that after 1908 it might "consider the qualifications of the teaching staff" in grant-aided Secondary schools, and:

> require that a certain proportion of new appointments shall consist of persons who have gone through a course of training recognised by the Board for this purpose.[1]

In 1908 the Board issued its first *Regulations for the Training of Teachers for Secondary Schools*. These did not include any requirement that a proportion of staff must be trained; they simply specified what forms of training would be recognised. In brief, training could be conducted in a University Training Department (UTD), a Training College, or a Teacher Training Department of a Secondary school. It would be restricted to graduates and 'graduate-equivalents', must last for one academic year, consist solely of professional training, and include (1) a special study of at least one subject in the Secondary school curriculum, and (2) at least 60 days of school practice, of which two-thirds or more must be in a Secondary school approved for the purpose by the Board.

The Board evidently did not expect a large initial response; it offered only £5,000 in grant for the first year. In the event, it had to pay out only £1,900; to ten training establishments, of which five were day training colleges. Over and above the unwillingness of men to train, there were several obstacles to rapid progress. The Board insisted that a training establishment must present at least ten students, and paid grant only on complete units of five. This particularly hampered Secondary school departments; so also did the requirement that at least half of the staff must have had successful experience of some length. UTDs and training colleges often had difficulty in finding enough Secondary schools "thoroughly suitable for demonstration and practice", as required by the Regulations. Training colleges also had difficulty about the special study of Secondary school subjects; they were not staffed for the purpose, and so were forced to appoint additional members of staff, frequently for mere handfuls of students. Some colleges attempted to lessen their problems by delegating the supervision of teaching practice to schools, but that was only possible when there were available Secondary schools which were both capable and willing to undertake this responsibility. Many schools were not capable; others, though capable were not willing, because they felt that "children must necessarily suffer when students in training are allowed to practise in schools"—a not unreasonable belief, however much the Board might assert that it had "no adequate foundation".[2]

The number of Secondary school teachers trained up to 1914 averaged under 200 a year, of whom about 160 were women.

Special Schools

In 1898 a Departmental Committee recommended that only teachers aged twenty-one or more, who had had experience in ordinary schools and had undergone special training, should be appointed to posts in Special schools. No action followed until 1908, when the Board of Education issued Regulations which allowed two-year trained teachers to have a third year in which to train for service in Special schools. The Board had to admit, however, that salaries in Special schools were not good enough "to ensure a supply of fully qualified Certificated teachers who have been trained for three years". So, as a temporary measure, it made available a two-year course which would qualify a man or woman as a Certificated teacher in one type of Special school. A teacher thus Certificated who transferred to an ordinary school would be recognised for one year as an uncertificated teacher, and thereafter could secure the Certificate by passing an examination in the Principles of Teaching.

In 1907 the voluntary associations concerned with the teaching of blind people jointly established an examining body: the College of Teachers of the Blind. The Board of Education promptly recognised the College, and gave added force to its recognition by including in its 1908 Regulations a requirement that teachers in Special schools for blind or deaf children must within two years secure an approved qualification for such work.[3]

The associations concerned with the teaching of the deaf were, unfortunately, unable to resolve their differences. Their two small training colleges, Fitzroy Square and Ealing, continued to work independently, and to become increasingly ineffective, until 1915. Then, following the death of St John Ackers, the two main associations amalgamated. They transferred all their training of teachers to Fitzroy Square, but it remained there for only four years more. In 1919 the 'National Association for the Oral Instruction of the Deaf', and its training college, were incorporated in the Education Faculty of Manchester University, to form a department under the direction of Miss Irene Goldsack (later, Lady (Alexander) Ewing). It was the beginning of a new, and infinitely happier and more successful era.

Art Schools

A common defect in all the schemes for the training of specialist teachers of art, said the Board of Education in its report for 1910–11, was that they made "no provision for securing either the general education or the professional training which are now generally agreed to be desirable for teachers".[4] In 1911 the Board appointed a Standing Committee of Advice for Education in Art, and devised a new Certificate for specialist teachers of art. To secure this Certificate, candidates had to produce evidence of proficiency in general education, and in professional training for the teaching of drawing and one other art subject. Because of the outbreak of war in 1914 the first examinations for this Certificate were not held until 1915.

Long before that the Royal College of Art had begun to introduce educational theory and professional training for teaching into its full-time courses for prospective teachers of art. In 1911 its first-year students were given lectures on Rousseau, Pestalozzi, and Froebel, instruction in the teaching of drawing in Elementary and Secondary schools, and teaching practice, at first in the college, and later in Elementary schools.

Domestic Subjects

In 1907 the Board of Education's Regulations provided for the payment of the teacher training grant to the Domestic Subjects colleges, a long overdue act of justice. What brought this about, however, was not justice but the state of the nation's health. Between 1902 and 1906 the Government had held investigations into the employment, medical condition, and nutrition of Elementary school children, and into the teaching of physical education in schools and training colleges. The reports produced had caused considerable concern; but it was the *Report of the Inter-Departmental Committee on Physical Deterioration,* published in 1904, which brought matters to a head.

This report, the result of an inquiry into why so many men wishing to serve in the Boer War had been rejected because of ill-health or physical defect, revealed that both were widespread in Britain, not least among children. Much could be done to improve matters by better medical and nutritional care of the young, it said. Among other recommendations it suggested that instruction in cookery, domestic economy, and hygiene should be made compulsory for older girls in Public Elementary schools, and that home management and hygiene should receive more attention in training colleges.

Morant asked the newly-established Women's Branch of HM Inspectorate to make a thorough inquiry into the work of all Schools of Cookery recognised by the Board for the training of teachers. On the whole, the Schools came well out of this, and were consequently offered *per capita* grants of up to £12 a head—far more than they had ever received before. There were, of course, conditions, the principal ones being that:

1 Students being trained as teachers must be enrolled in separate classes.

2 Grant would be paid only on students who successfully completed a two-year Diploma course.

3 The increased amount of grant was to be used to bring premises, staffing, equipment, and the quality of the instruction to the

ST PATRICK'S COLLEGE LIBRARY

higher level of efficiency which the Board will in future look for as a condition of continued recognition under the new Regulations, whether for grants or Diplomas".[5]

While the Board was satisfied with the work of the Schools, it was far from satisfied with the examination for the Diploma. It thought too little attention was being paid to general science, the foundation for domestic science. It therefore required that from 1908 the examination should be divided into three parts: (1) the Special Subject, i.e. cookery, housewifery, or laundry; (2) Theory of Education; and (3) Science.

In the succeeding years some weaknesses became apparent in the Schools' work. Consequently, in 1912 and 1913 the Board had full inspections made of all the fourteen Schools recognised for the training of teachers. The results from these inspections suggested that a thorough overhaul was needed; not because the work of the Schools was bad, but because it differed so greatly from that of the general colleges. The Board came to the conclusion that the Diploma course in Domestic Subjects could not be combined with a Teacher's Certificate course—a feat which a few of the general colleges had attempted. The Domestic Subjects course must be done in a specialist college, and it must last a full two years.

In their report following the inspections HMI made various criticisms, of which the following were the most important.

1   The subjects in the (increasingly popular) 'Combined' course were being taken in the wrong order.

2   The 'Special' subjects were not correlated with the general science.

3   The Schools were not tackling the problems presented by the very various attainments in science of new entrants.

4   The teaching was too academic.

5   The subject matter taught had little relevance to the homes from which Elementary school children came.

The upshot was that the Combined course replaced the Special subjects courses. The Board's 1914 Regulations laid down that from August 1915 no students would be recognised for grant who had not entered for the two-year Combined course.

Physical Education

In 1906 the Board mounted an inquiry into the teaching of physical education in the residential training colleges. By the turn of the century this subject had become a normal item in the colleges' curriculum, but it was in general poorly taught and equipped. The Board's enquiry confirmed what many people already believed: that in most training colleges little attempt was made to explain systematically to students either the theory or the practice of physical education. The alarming reports about the nation's health had, however, begun to effect some improvements in facilities.

Handwork

Under the general heading of 'Handwork' were included in the early 1900s three very different types of activity.

1 Froebelian 'Hand and Eye Training', for young children.

2 'Light Crafts', e.g. basketry, for rather older children.

3 'Manual Instruction', i.e. woodwork and/or metalwork, for senior boys in Elementary schools.

Of these, Hand and Eye Training was by 1900 fairly common in the Infant Departments of Elementary schools. Its practice was, however, being criticised, in England notably by Dr Hughlings Jackson, who pointed out that the nerves and muscles controlling large movements developed earlier than those controlling small ones. Such Froebelian activities as "pricking and sewing, pea and stick work, the threading of small beads . . . fine and exact paper folding"[6] were being imposed upon children at too early an age, with consequent physical and educational harm.

This criticism caused a violent controversy among the English Froebelians, but Dr Jackson's views prevailed. They were upheld in 1904 by a team of women HMIs who investigated Infant education. The five Inspectors declared that children between the ages of three and five were getting "no profit intellectually from school instruction"; on the contrary, "the mechanical teaching which they often receive dulls their imagination and weakens their power of independent observation". The *Kindergarten* 'occupations' did not escape this criticism; they were, said HMI, "often distinguished by absence of occupation".[7]

The Froebel Society promptly revised their syllabus; in 1906 they replaced the 'Gifts and Occupations' by more appropriate educational handwork. Concurrently, they revised their examination scheme. Their Joint Examining Board, established in 1887, was incorporated in a National Froebel Union, which immediately raised the academic qualifications required for entry into a Froebel training college. From 1905 only holders of a School Certificate awarded by a university examining Board would be considered. The Union also encouraged students to aim at the Higher rather than the Lower Froebel Certificate. The effect of these changes was virtually to impose a three-year course upon students who wished to secure both the Board of Education and the Froebel Union Certificates.

Manual Instruction

Neither the training nor the status of manual instructors was greatly improved during the first decade of the twentieth century. Few training colleges were yet well enough staffed or equipped to teach woodwork or metalwork competently. To get a thorough training a teacher had to rely on the part-time courses and summer schools organised by some LEAs, the Educational Handwork Association, and the National Association of Manual Training Teachers, or go abroad, to Sweden, home of 'Slöjd',[8] or some other European country.

There was, however, one notable development during this decade: an experiment launched by the LCC at the Shoreditch Technical Institute. In 1905 the Council started a small number of pupil-teachers on a four-year full-time course of general education and specialised instruction in woodwork and metalwork. During the third and fourth years they were given teaching practice in Elementary schools. Those who successfully completed the course received the title of 'Junior Assistant Instructor in Handicrafts'. Out of this experiment was to be born Shoreditch Training College, the first college in the United Kingdom devoted to producing specialist teachers of woodwork and metalwork.

Music

Not much progress was made towards producing specialist teachers of music. Every training college prepared its students to teach singing, and most of them did this very thoroughly. At many there was also much instrumental music, with a widening range of instruments. But the specialist music teacher had yet to come.

References

1 *Report of the Board of Education 1906–1907*, p. 70.
2 *Report of the Board of Education 1912–1913*, pp. 176 and 177.
3 *Regulations for the Training of Teachers for Elementary Schools 1908*, Article 51 (i).
4 *Report of the Board of Education 1910–1911*, p. 60.
5 *Regulations for the Training of Teachers of Domestic Subjects 1907*, Prefatory Memorandum, p. iv.
6 Lawrence, Evelyn (ed.), *Friedrich Froebel and English Education*, University of London Press, 1952, p. 88.
7 *Report of the Board of Education 1904–1905*, p. 25.
8 *Slöjd* (literally, 'dexterity'; compare the English word 'sleight' in 'sleight of hand') was a system of wood carving with cultural aims. It was developed in Swedish schools during the last quarter of the nineteenth century by the philosopher August Abrahamson and his nephew Otto Salomon.

CHAPTER THIRTEEN

College Life in the early 1900s

"The students' social life in the first decade of the twentieth century," wrote Miss Olive Stanton, a former principal of Darlington Training College, "was lively, if still restricted."[1]

How lively? How restricted? What was it like to be a training college student in that decade? It depended considerably, of course, on where you were. To trek daily to and from a day training college in a grimy industrial town—and industrial towns were *very* grimy in those days—was a vastly different matter from being a member of a residential college in a pleasant rural district.

It is difficult to present a comprehensive picture of student life during those years, because the evidence is patchy, with domestic matters in particular getting scant attention. This chapter contains, therefore, no more than a few heterogeneous gleanings.

To members of residential establishments the food is always of prime interest. The 1904 Regulations for the training of teachers contained an appendix on 'Dietary'. In this the Board of Education suggested that students should have four meals a day: breakfast, dinner, tea, and supper. Dinner should be the main meal, but meat, eggs, or fish should be provided at one other meal, preferably breakfast. The purpose of supper was, according to the Board, "not so much to provide nourishment as to withdraw into the digestive area the blood from the brain excited by study".

The daily allowance of meat, including bone, should be not less than 12 oz. for men, 10 oz. for women. Only "fresh prime" meat should be used, and none should be twice cooked. The allowances of fish should be half as heavy again. There should be "a liberal supply of bread and potatoes, daily fresh vegetables, or salad, or raw fruit".

How did this work out in practice? Four meals a day: yes. Midday dinner the main meal: yes. Here, for example, is the dinner menu at the Derby Diocesan Training College posted up in September 1900.

Sunday	Cold roast beef Fruit pies or jam tarts
Monday	Hot roast beef Boiled rice with jam or syrup
Tuesday	Soup Cold Meat
Wednesday	Roast veal (summer) or roast pork (winter)
	Stewed fruit or boiled fruit puddings
Thursday	Roast leg of mutton Cheese
Friday	Fish Boiled jam or syrup pudding
Saturday	Hashed meat or joints Rice or sago pudding[2]

No mention is made of vegetables; one assumes these were taken for granted.

Opinions about the diet at Derby varied. The authorities, predictably, said it was "remarkably" good. The students (equally predictably) described it as "poor". They particularly criticised the breakfasts, not without reason, apparently, for a new, presumably improved, menu was shortly introduced, as follows:

Sunday, Wednesday, and Friday
   Coffee, bread and butter with marmalade and jam, or egg
Monday, Tuesday, Thursday, and Saturday
   Coffee, bread and bacon, marmalade and jam[3]

At Westminster Training College, until 1903 (or possibly later) both breakfast and tea consisted of bread and butter only, with coffee or tea. Students had, however, a reasonably substantial supper: milk, cheese, bread and butter.

About men's clothes college histories and magazines say almost nothing. But they say quite a lot about women's.

It was an age of transition. Throughout the nineteenth century the rule had been absolute: "the utmost simplicity of dress and modesty of demeanour".[4] In the early 1900s this tradition was still strong, but its extremeist rigours were being at least marginally relaxed. At Derby, before 1900, the students were "allowed to have flowers under the brims of their hats but not on top".[5]

At Darlington:
   Students were expected to wear a dark costume (preferably

blue), a white blouse with a College tie, and to bring a white
dress for "occasions".[6]

At Warrington:

> In the years 1903–05 a typical Warrington Training College
> student wore, ordinarily, a black or navy ankle-length skirt, a
> neat blouse with high neck and long sleeves and a distinguishing
> white sailor (or boater) straw hat with a black band bearing the
> College monogram. The Drill outfit consisted of a navy pleated
> skirt with sailor blouse and white front, and rubber shoes. For
> Science a black overall was worn and for Needlework a white
> apron with bib—the latter such as a parlour maid of those days
> would wear. Hair was piled up on top of the head or in a 'bun' at
> the back. Short hair styles were unknown.[7]

When, ten years later, a Municipal Training College was opened
at Hull, the women were:

> burdened with hideous black serge tunics, adorned with violent
> yellow velvet saddles and girdles; and cream straw boaters with
> hat bands of the same wasplike colours.

"In these," says the writer:

> with the huge black bows we wore in our hair whenever we
> could elude the disapproving eyes of the women staff, and the
> long, extremely tight hobble skirts of the day, we must have
> rivalled any absurd student fashion of the last fifty years![8]

"Elude the disapproving eyes of the women staff . . ." The words
give insight into relations between students and staff. Much more
astonishing were the relations authority attempted to impose on men
and women students. At Hull there was to be "no speaking to the
opposite sex". At Goldsmiths' in the early days there were separate
entrances, separate common rooms, even separate classes. "We were a
new venture," explained a vice-principal, "and had to be cautious."[9]

It was only towards the end of the nineteenth century that students'
common rooms became the rule rather than the exception. At
Lincoln there was none until 1903. Study bedrooms were still
comparatively rare; students slept in dormitories, which were usually
divided into 'cubicles'. At Warrington:

> Each cubicle occupied a very narrow space entered by drawing aside a green curtain, and containing a hard wooden bed attached at one side to the partition separating the cubicles. There was a small dressing table with drawers and a small washstand with washbasin and a jug of white china. Each student filled her jug from a tap somewhere along the corridor.[10]

A cold tap, of course; hot water in dormitories was virtually unknown.

Culham had no students' common room until 1902, and no students' bathrooms until 1907. At Westminster there were until 1906, when the premises were modernised, neither bathrooms nor washbasins; only a "long wooden trough in the basement".[11]

Nevertheless, during these years the social life in residential colleges began to burgeon into richness and variety. At Derby there were by 1906 several flourishing sports clubs: hockey, badminton, tennis, 'spiropole' (a predecessor of netball). During the following five years debating, dramatic, and literary societies were formed. At Goldsmiths' staff initiatives led to a Howard club, a debating society, and an Old Students' Association. At Sheffield, as the men had no common room, the principal gave them the use of the College hall on Saturday evenings for "dances, socials and debates"—to which women could come—and once a fortnight on Tuesdays for a 'smoker'—to which women could *not* come.[12]

The earliest LEA colleges were very variously housed. Hereford and Sheffield took over the premises of boarding schools, Fulham the building of a Higher Grade Elementary school. Avery Hill inherited a mansion set in a spacious park. Brighton's teaching and residential accommodation, both urban, were a mile apart.

The pattern of a student's day was largely determined by whether the college was residential or non-residential. In most residential colleges work began early and ended late. At Warrington, for example, where (as in many colleges) the day was regulated by the ringing of bells, the first of these was at 6.15 am, the last at 9.30 pm. An hour or so of lecture, tests, or private study before breakfast was usual. Classes occupied the morning from 9.30 to one. Thanks largely to persistent pressure from HM Inspectorate, by the beginning of the twentieth century the afternoons had in many residential colleagues been freed of classes. These started again after tea (taken about 4 to

4.30), and continued ordinarily for about two hours. Before or after supper, and in some colleges before *and* after, there was private study or preparation of lessons for the following day. In church colleges the day would include two or more chapel services. With such regimes, it is hardly surprising to find HMI commending students not only as well-behaved and industrious, but also as 'docile'.

Day training colleges usually worked an eight-hour day, from nine to five or so. In addition, students would have private study in the evening, at home, lodgings, or hostel. For students living in hostels the evenings as well as the days were regulated by the college authorities. At Sheffield—probably quite typically—classes began at 9 am, continued until one, and, except on two afternoons a week given to sport, went on again from two to 4.30. Residential students were then free for one hour, but had to be back in their hostel for tea. *No one was allowed out after tea!* Private study occupied the time between six and eight, except on Saturdays and Sundays.

In both day and residential colleges most of the classes were devoted to lectures. The quality of these naturally varied, but it is probably safe to say that the majority were conscientious, serious, and staid to the point of dullness. Not all would be scholarly, but some would be pedantic. Newly-established colleges often found it difficult to get good staff, and some had to rely largely upon part-timers. Some, even among the older colleges, had few graduates on their staff. Lincoln had none (except the principal) until 1904.

A traditional feature of all college curricula was the 'Crit'—the 'Criticism Lesson'. Mr Adam Rankine, HMI, described it in his 1902 report.

> Some days before the appointed time the student who is to teach brings a rough outline of the proposed lesson to the officer of the staff who is going to hear it, and receives general advice and suggestions. Detailed guidance is purposely withheld in order that the student may be encouraged to think for himself. After further consideration the student draws up a sketch of the lesson and posts it up publicly, so that everyone who is to be present may copy it and have time to think it over. The lesson lasts usually about half an hour. and discussion and criticism follow it for an hour. All the conditions of real work are observed. As soon as the lesson is over and the children dismissed, full and free

criticism is encouraged. The various points—matter, method, manner, illustrations, language, power of questioning, and all the little touches and devices or art by which mistakes are corrected, discipline maintained, and interest quickened are submitted to searching investigation. Faults are pointed out and remedies suggested. The criticism is unsparing but free from malice. It is curative and formative. It aims at improvement and endeavours to bring to light the perfect method. The members of the staff who have been present then offer their observations and the whole is concluded by the President, frequently the Principal, who sums up.[13]

"It is an ordeal for the beginner," commented Mr Rankine. To many students it was a nightmare. Its weaknesses were its extreme artificiality, the myth it fostered that there was a perfect mode of teaching, and, worst of all, the acute distress it caused so many students.

With an increased emphasis on professional training, the amount of time given to teaching practice grew longer. In the earlier years the Board of Education's Regulations specified that two-year students were "not in any case required to spend more than three weeks [a year] in class teaching", but in 1906 this was altered to "must spend three weeks".[14] Three-year students were to have a total of eight weeks, not six as previously. During these years the location of teaching practice also altered. Before the 1902 Act most teaching practice in the residential colleges took place in their 'Model', 'Practising', or 'Demonstration' schools, and even day training colleges, which did not own such schools, got into the habit of using only one Elementary school.

The 1902 Act completely altered the position by placing all Elementary schools under the administrative control of the LEAs. This meant that the residential colleges no longer had an unrestricted right to use particular schools. The Board of Education made it a condition of grant to an Elementary school that it must accept students for teaching practice, but would not sanction "any arrangement likely to interfere with the school's efficiency or put any undue burden on the teachers".[15] This largely ended the almost perpetual occupation of a school by training college staff and students.

But the habit of using one school only continued in some places for

many years. Lincoln opened in 1904 new premises for its Girls'
Practising School; they were used for practice until 1930. In 1913 the
Hull Higher Education Committee selected a single school to provide
teaching practice facilities for the newly-established Municipal
Training College, including sending children to the college for
demonstration lessons. This arrangement lasted until 1941—and it
was the Second World War that ended it.

Many day training colleges did all or most of their teaching
practice during the university vacations. Many Voluntary and LEA
colleges divided the required six weeks into three periods of two
weeks each. The first was devoted to teaching the basic subjects, and
the second the 'class' subjects; the third was spent correcting faults
and remedying weaknesses. Some colleges were less systematic; at
Warrington, for example, according to a 1903–5 student:

> Very little practical teaching was included in our curriculum. In
> the first year one week at a local practising school and a few odd
> lessons were the sum total. During the Summer holidays at the
> end of the first year we spent a fortnight for observation at a
> school of our own choice and with the approval of the Education
> Committee and the co-operation of the Head Teacher ... We
> submitted a comprehensive report on our return to college. In
> the second year we had three consecutive weeks in schools.[16]

In this instance the teaching practice was doubtless enjoyable, for the
Head and the staff "spared no effort to make our visit a success". But
in general it must have been a time of strain. Those were the days
when:

> classes were large and methods and discipline often rigid. The
> teachers of that generation had themselves been in charge of
> classes of 80 as pupil-teachers in their 'teens': hence there was a
> good deal of 'Eyes on teacher,' 'Pens down' and 'Left-Right' ...
> The children, whatever their size or shape, were crammed into
> double desks with sloping tops, unsuitable for handwork, or
> indeed for anything but the three Rs. In those days the whole
> conception of education was instructional and disciplinary; the
> Play Way had not come into being.[17]

Yet some of the teaching practice procedures of the early 1900s were
not unlike some of those of the 1970s.

Before entering the school each student is furnished with a copy
of the class timetable, and a syllabus of the lessons which will
have to be given ... A notebook must be kept, and in it must be
entered such items as a general plan of the school, detailed
sketches of the classrooms, a description and criticism of the
general arrangements of the school, its ventilation, lighting, etc.
Teaching notes of all lessons, and full notes of selected lessons are
given, and at the close of each day observations on the work
done are recorded, success or failure is noted, and some attempt
is made to ascertain the cause. Character studies of children who
present peculiarities of a marked kind are not omitted.[18]

Visits for observation were equally carefully organised.

Some of the best and some of the worst schools, Secondary
Schools and schools for defectives, schools in rich and schools in
poor neighbourhoods are carefully studied. These visits afterwards form the subjects of papers, in which observations are
recorded and results summarised.[19]

"... some of the worst ..." Realism indeed, as anyone who was a
pupil or a teacher in an Elementary school in the early 1900s can
testify.

References

1 Stanton, Olive M, *Our Present Opportunities*: The History of Darlington
  College of Education (Darlington Training College), published by the
  author, 1966, p. 96.
2 Quoted from Dobson, Margaret, *The History of the First Hundred Years of the
  Diocesan Training College, Derby*, published by the College, 1951, p. 38.
3 ibid., p. 37.
4 ibid., p. 20.
5 ibid., p. 37.
6 Stanton, op. cit. p. 96.
7 Letter, dated 8 May 1958, from Miss Ellen Parkinson to Miss M A B
  Jones, then principal of St Katharine's College, Liverpool.
8 Miss D W Farrer, quoted in *The First Fifty Years*: A Brief History of
  Kingston upon Hull Training College, 1913–1963, edited by C B, and
  published by the College, 1963, p. 17.
9 Dymond, *op. cit.* p. 96. Miss Caroline Graveson, whose words these were,
  was joint vice-principal from the opening of the College in 1905 until
  1934.

10　From the letter mentioned in Note 7.

11　Pritchard, F C, *The Story of Westminster College 1851–1951*, Epworth Press, 1951, p. 77.

12　Millington, Roy, *A History of the City of Sheffield Training College,* published by the College, 1955, p. 29.

13　*General Reports of HM Inspectors on Elementary Schools and Training Colleges for the Year 1902*, p. 167.

14　*Regulations for the Training of Teachers and for the Examination of Students in Training Colleges 1906*, Article 34.

15　*Regulations for the Training of Teachers and for the Examination of Students in Training Colleges 1904*, Appendix F.

16　From the letter mentioned in Note 7.

17　*Furzedown College 1908–1958,* published by the College, 1958, p. 10.

18　Mr Adam Rankine, in *General Reports of HM Inspectors on Elementary Schools and Training Colleges for the Year 1902*, pp. 169–70.

19　ibid., p. 170.

CHAPTER FOURTEEN

The Impact of War

Within a few weeks of the outbreak of war in August 1914 nearly one-third of the men training to be teachers in England and Wales were in the Armed Forces. By January 1915 nearly half were. In 1916 conscription was introduced; thereafter, no men fit for service in the Forces could be accepted for training. By 1918 the number of men students was under one-tenth of the 1914 figure.

Several of the Voluntary colleges disintegrated on the day war was declared, because most of their students, and many of the staff, were members of the Territorial Army, and were mobilised at once. Bede (Durham), St John's (Battersea), and Winchester lost over 90 per cent, Culham (Oxfordshire) 80 per cent. Some of the day training colleges were similarly depleted. Elsewhere, numbers fell sharply as men rushed enthusiastically to enlist.

The buildings of several of the colleges were requisitioned. Amalgamations resulted. The few remaining students at St Mark's (Chelsea) moved into St John's. St Gabriel's, a women's college in south London, went to Culham, whose remaining handful of students was distributed among other Anglican colleges. Westminster and Borough Road were forced into exile, as were the LEA colleges at Leeds, Manchester, and Sheffield.

In all the men's colleges it was for months a matter of living a day at a time. Until November 1915 the decision whether or not to enlist was a personal one; then, the Board of Education said, in Circular 928, that the need to increase the Armed Forces was "paramount", and that all physically fit men should enlist.

In the women's colleges the situation was completely different. Women were urged to become teachers. The buildings were not requisitioned. In many colleges life continued very much as before until 1916, except that leisure-time activities became increasingly directed towards aiding the war effort. During the second half of the war life became much less comfortable for all, and acutely uncomfortable for some. Colleges in eastern England were liable to be harassed by Zeppelins—an entirely new form of warfare, and therefore doubly terrifying to many people. At Hull, where "the crowds streaming out for safety from the city's centre" used to shelter under the high wall of the Municipal Training College, there was one "terrible week when the Zeppelins came and returned over Hull six nights out of seven".[1] It happened also to be the week of the practical teaching examination.

To what extent academic and professional standards in the colleges deteriorated during the war is difficult to determine; there seems to be almost a conspiracy of silence about it in contemporary documents. Obviously, standards varied according to circumstances. It is probably safe to say that in the women's colleges they did not fall markedly during the first half of the war; about the second half one cannot feel so confident. The few men in the colleges from 1916 onwards were all medically much below average, and so should not perhaps be assessed by normal criteria.

Though more young people joined the teaching profession during the war than might have been expected, it became increasingly clear that when it was over large numbers of additional teachers would be required. Recruitment had been sagging badly before 1914. The appalling slaughter on the Western front was tearing huge gaps in the ranks of the nation's young men. And from 1916 it was obvious that the demand for more education, at all levels, was growing.

The Board of Education acknowledged that:

> after the war it will not suffice merely to repair the losses which education has suffered ... improvements and development of our existing system are essential to the national welfare.

and declared itself:

> alive to the necessity of taking all possible steps to prepare for any opportunity which may arise of giving practical effect to it by suitable legislation or administrative action.[2]

It had long before taken action to safeguard the interests of the students in college or enlisted. In November 1914, in response to recommendations from the training college principals, it had made, in Circular 878, the following statement:

1 For students whose training would ordinarily have been completed in July 1915, but who wished to join the Forces earlier, a special examination would be held at Easter. Successful candidates would be immediately awarded the Teacher's Certificate.

2 Students in their second (or a later) year of training who had already joined the Forces would have a choice of two alternatives:

   (i) they could return to college after the war and complete their training; *or*

   (ii) provided that (a) they had served in the Forces for at least one year, and (b) were recommended by their College, they could be granted temporary recognition as Certificated Teachers without further training or examination. This recognition would hold good for the first two years of service; then, provided satisfactory reports were received from HMI and the employing LEA, it would be made permanent.

When conscription was introduced in 1916 the Board undertook to grant temporary recognition as Certificated Teachers to students unable to complete their first year of training, provided that they returned to college after the war for a six months' course which would concentrate upon academic rather than professional studies. Permanent recognition would be granted after two years' satisfactory service as a teacher.[3]

The problem of wartime staffing was largely met by waiving paper qualifications and recruiting any men or women who seemed likely to do reasonably good work. A few of these people were given short training courses; the LCC, for example, in 1915 offered a twelve-week course to 100 women willing to teach in Infant schools. In the same year the Manchester LEA organised a much longer course, a one-year full-time course, for women Certificated teachers wishing to teach in Special schools for mentally handicapped children. This course, which consisted largely of practical activities—drawing, housecraft, hygiene, gardening, and physical exercises—and a similar one held at Furzedown College in London, led to significant developments. An HMI report suggested that such courses could be used to train teachers for ordinary Elementary schools; and from that suggestion the idea evolved that ex-service men and women might thus be trained.

In 1916 the Board of Education approved a scheme submitted by Southampton University College for providing vocational training to disabled soldiers. In 1917 it approved a more academic scheme proposed by the University College of Wales, and agreed provisionally to an LCC proposal to establish at the Shoreditch Technical Institute a two-year course leading to the Teacher's Certificate which would "lay special emphasis upon practical and manual work". It commented that "courses of such kind may be found suitable for a certain number of men who are discharged from the Army".[4]

Within a few months courses of similar character were being organised at Liverpool University and elsewhere. They were longer courses—usually two-year—and they comprised both academic study and professional training, with particular emphasis upon the principles and practice of teaching. Candidates were selected by specially appointed committees, representative of HM Inspectorate, the LEAs, the training colleges, and the teachers' professional associations. Provided that an applicant's general health and physical capacity were good, physical defects—even the loss of a limb—did not preclude admission into training.

It soon became evident that there was no reason to restrict entry into such courses to men who had been invalided out of the Forces. As soon as the war ended, comparable courses were organised for normally fit ex-service men by, for example, the Lancashire and Manchester LEAs and the University of Sheffield. The Lancashire course, held at Lancaster, was perhaps the most interesting. Housed in the Storey Institute (a Junior Art and Technical College), it was non-residential. Its students were of all ages from 19 to 40. The curriculum closely resembled that of an ordinary training college, but the day-to-day life, the discipline, and the relations between staff and students were vastly different. Work was sustained by mutual enthusiasm, discipline by mutual agreement.

Another scheme, for the training of specialist teachers of handicrafts, became much larger than had been anticipated. It evolved out of a vocational training project launched by the Ministry of Labour during the war. Many of the applicants for this were skilled craftsmen; and someone suggested that they might make good teachers. The Ministry, after consulting the Board of Education, agreed to try out an experimental training course for teaching, at Sarisbury Court, near Southampton, one of its training centres. Although the course was to last (including vacations) for over eighteen months, it attracted more than 3,000 applicants. Additional courses were arranged, by the Ministry of Labour in London, Manchester, and Kent, and by the Board of Education in the training colleges at Chester, Crewe, Exeter, and Winchester, and at Southampton University College. Although the failure rate was rather high, about 1,000 men were successfully trained.

One happy development due in part to the success of these courses was a rise in the status of handicraft teachers in both Elementary and Secondary schools. To this development the Board of Education contributed by persisting with its campaign, begun before the war, to get handicrafts taught in schools by Certificated teachers, and not by craftsmen untrained as teachers, however skilled they might be at their trade.

Alongside these officially organised experiments went a number of private ones. Three of these, all concerned with the education of young children, were to prove very valuable. In 1917 Miss Belle Rennie, secretary of the Conference of New Ideals (out of which was to grow the New Education Fellowship), with the aid of a group of her friends opened at Gipsy Hill in south-east London a training college for teachers of children between the ages of two and seven. About the same time a similar college was opened in Manchester. The Board of Education at first viewed these colleges with caution. It considered their methods "somewhat novel" (which they were), and refused to grant their students full recognition.

> Students who complete courses at these colleges will in the first instance only be recognised provisionally as Certificated-Teachers ... their Certificates will be subject to confirmation after two years' actual experience in teaching.[5]

In 1918 Goldsmiths' College opened a Nursery school designed as a

Demonstration school for students wishing to teach children under the age of five in Infant schools. In its early days this school worked in close co-operation with, and received valuable assistance from, the Welfare Committee of nearby Deptford, where only a few years previously Margaret and Rachel McMillan had opened the first Nursery school in England. The Goldsmiths' College school was used by students for observation and practice until 1940, when evacuation put an end to it.

In 1919 the McMillans' Nursery school was recognised by the Board of Education as a training centre for students wishing to be Nursery school teachers. Margaret McMillan had, in fact, anticipated official recognition several months earlier by putting up a notice which read: 'Rachel McMillan Training Centre and Open Air Nursery School'. (Her sister Rachel had died in 1917; this was to be her memorial.) For ten years Centre and School had to co-exist in the School's buildings, but in 1930, thanks largely to help from Lady (Nancy) Astor, who believed passionately in the value of nursery education, and from her husband, Viscount Astor, the Rachel McMillan Training College was opened alongside the Nursery school—as Margaret had always insisted it must be.

References

1 Miss C T Cumberbirch, acting principal at the time, quoted in *The First Fifty Years*, p. 20.
2 *Report of the Board of Education 1915–16*, pp. 2–3.
3 *Report of the Board of Education 1916–17*, p. 66.
4 ibid., p. 64.
5 ibid.

CHAPTER FIFTEEN

New Initiatives

In December 1916 the Prime Minister, Mr David Lloyd George, invited the Vice-Chancellor of Sheffield University, Mr H A L Fisher, to become President of the Board of Education. He did so because, according to Fisher, he felt that:

> we had now reached a point in our history when the country would take more educational reform from an educationalist than from a politician.[1]

Fisher had no mind to play a passive role. "Would there be money for educational reforms and improvements?" he asked. Lloyd George promised that there would, and that he would give the President his personal support.[2] Fortified by these assurances, in 1918 Fisher piloted through Parliament an Education Act and a Teachers Superannuation Act, both of which embodied substantial reforms, and in 1919 ended the worst anomalies in teachers' pay by establishing national salary scales—the 'Burnham' scales.

About the two Acts of Parliament the Board of Education commented that:

> Before the war the passage of these measures would have been difficult, but it was made easy by the determination of all classes of the people that effect should be given to a larger and more generous view of the public responsibility in the sphere of education.[3]

That was no exaggeration. The closing months of the First World War saw in England a widespread enthusiasm for the extension and improvement of public education. The sorry tale of how that enthusiasm was to shrivel in the icy blasts of 'national economy' is too well known to need repetition here. But for a year or two after the Armistice optimism prevailed.

The Government gave high priority to the demobilisation of teachers. The Board of Education quickly put into operation plans for the recruitment and training of teachers which it had been maturing throughout the war. The response was even better than had been hoped; such large numbers of men applied for training that by 1920 the training colleges and UTDs were full to overflowing.

That being so, it is surprising to find the Church of England thinking of closing some of its colleges. But the war had decimated their incomes, and a Comission appointed by the Archbishops in 1916 had recommended a policy of 'concentration'—which meant in blunter words selling some colleges and using the funds thus acquired to help the others back to solvency. The supporters of the threatened colleges, however, resisted so strongly that no college was closed, though the ancient colleges of St Mark and St John were amalgamated.

In 1920 the first national economy drive began. In December a Select Committee of the House of Commons criticised what it considered inadequate control of expenditure on public education. In January 1921 Fisher, under orders from the Treasury, issued Circular 1190 telling LEAs not to incur, or commit themselves to incurring, any new expenditure. In August the Government, goaded by allegations that it was not effecting enough economies, appointed a 'Business Men's Committee' (the 'Geddes' Committee) to consider "reductions in the national expenditure on supply services". This Committee reported in February 1922, proposing reductions too drastic for the Government to stomach. In education they included raising the age of entry from five to six, increasing the size of classes, and reducing teachers' salaries. The cuts the Government made were bad enough; among their immediate results was some unemployment among teachers fresh from training college.

Troubles mounted. In 1921 Fisher learned that LEAs providing training colleges had been advised by their professional associations to close their colleges unless they got better grants. Fortunately, he was able to avert a crisis by securing substantial increases. But that did not solve the fundamental problem: that the LEAs maintaining training colleges bore the entire cost of these, and the other LEAs got their teachers trained free.

Unfortunately, the LEAs were divided about how to solve this problem. Some argued (as did many teachers) that training should be a national service, wholly financed by the Government. Others held that the cost of training should be met out of a 'pool' to which all LEAs had to contribute on some equitable basis. The Board of Education did not like either of these plans; it believed that LEAs should join up in groups to support individual colleges. Discussions between the Board and the LEAs proved abortive, but in 1925 a Departmental Committee on the training of teachers (of which more later) came down in favour of a 'pool', and the Government accepted its recommendation that:

> Grants payable in respect of Training Colleges provided by LEAs should be paid on the same basis as grants paid to other (i.e. Voluntary) colleges. The additional expenditure consequently incurred by the Exchequer should be regarded as a sum to be recovered by equitable apportionment among the Local Education Authorities for Higher Education which do not provide Training Colleges.[4]

The recommendation was incorporated in the Economy (Miscellaneous Provisions) Act 1926. Regulations made under this Act provided that the Higher Education grants payable to a local authority not providing a training college (other than a Domestic Subjects college) in 1926–27 would be reduced by a sum equal in aggregate to the sum of the 'additional grants' payable to local authorities providing training colleges, the amount of the levy being determined by reference to the average attendance in its Public elementary schools and the rateable value of the area.[5]

Financial troubles were not the only cause of unease in the training colleges during the years immediately following the war. Academic and professional problems also abounded. Was a longer course necessary? Should the course for non-graduates be, like that for graduates, wholly professional? Should all teachers be graduates? Was there in the college course too much emphasis on academic education, and too little on professional training? What minimum academic attainment should be required of entrants into college? Should prospective teachers stay at school until they entered training college, or should they do a spell of student-teaching between school and college? Should the training colleges be incorporated in, or associated with, universities or university colleges? And so on.

In March 1923 the President of the Board of Education, Mr Edward Wood (later Lord Halifax), appointed a Departmental Committee, under the chairmanship of Viscount Burnham:

> To review the arrangements for the Training of Teachers for Public Elementary Schools, and to consider what changes, if any, in the organisation or finance of the existing system are desirable in order that a supply of well-qualified teachers adjustable to the demands of the schools may be secured, regard being had to:
>
> (a) the economy of public funds;
> (b) the attractions offered to young persons as compared with other professions and occupations;
> (c) the facilities afforded by Secondary Schools and Universities for acquiring academic qualifications.

The training of teachers for Secondary schools was unfortunately not included in the Committee's terms of reference. This omission effectively prevented it from making the comprehensive review of all aspects of teacher training which the President had promised. Its report also suffered from being far from unanimous. Four of the eighteen members of the Committee did not sign it (though they agreed with much that it contained), and six made 'Notes of Reservation'. Nevertheless, it led to many reforms.

The Report contained 69 recommendations. Among the more important were:

1 Aid from public funds should continue to be made to young people who intend to become teachers.

2 The ultimate objective of the Board of Education should be the recognition of none but Certificated teachers.

3 Evidence of the successful completion of an approved course of training should be required as a condition of recognition as a teacher in a Public Elementary school.

4 So far as is practicable, intending teachers should receive their secondary education in a Secondary school.

5 Pupil-Teachership and Student-Teachership should be discouraged.

6 As the essential function of the Training College is to train students to become effective teachers, its courses of training should be organised primarily with that end in view.

7 The minimum academic qualification for entry into Training College should be a School Certificate and evidence of at least one year's study in school after obtaining it.

8 The Training College course should extend over not less than two years, and the opportunities offered by a third year be more used.

9 Courses extending over two or three years which comprised a degree course and professional training should cease to be recognised as qualifying for the Teacher's Certificate.

10 The establishment should be encouraged of examining boards, representative of Universities and Governing Bodies of Training Colleges, to examine the students of a College or a group of Colleges, for the purpose of the recognition of the students by the Board of Education as Certificated Teachers.

11 The Board of Education's Regulations should cease to distinguish between Elementary and Secondary courses of training.

12 Training College students' maintenance allowances should rank for grant.

13 Exchequer grants to LEA colleges should be paid on the same basis as those to Voluntary colleges. The additional expenditure incurred by the Exchequer should be recovered by equitable apportionment among the LEAs for Higher Education which do not provide Training Colleges.

Reactions to the Report were mixed. The LEAs, while approving much in it, did not like the "costly" plan" of maintaining pupils up to the age of eighteen who then went straight from school to training college. *The Schoolmaster,* reflecting the view of the NUT, called the Report "A Disappointing Document". The Committee, it said, had failed to seize the opportunity to make substantial reforms in the training of teachers. In particular, it had retained "the dual function of the training college as a place of academic education (but with a lower limit of attainment) and professional training", and so had offered no more than "a feeble compromise which renders the academic side anaemic and the professional side no more robust".[6]

The Schoolmaster wanted the plan proposed in the 'Memorandum of Dissent' to the Report, which was signed by (among others) the two representatives of the NUT. This advocated a one- or two-year course of solely professional training, available only to graduates, or non-graduates with a Higher School Certificate. It also recommended that the Government should meet that part of the cost of a training college which came from public funds.

The Board of Education agreed in principle with the recommendations in the main Report, and at once implemented several of them. It abolished from 1927 the Acting Teacher's Certificate, and from 1928 the Preliminary Examination for the Certificate; thereafter all applicants to training colleges, except rural pupil-teachers, must have a School Certificate. And it invited the training colleges to send it their ideas about joint examining boards.

Not everyone wanted such boards; but in a series of conferences arranged by the Board of Education between March 1926 and May 1928 a scheme was hammered out. There would be eleven regional groups of training colleges, each linked with a university or university college. Each region would have its joint examining board, which would frame and conduct examinations in academic subjects and the theory of education. The Board of Education would continue to assess practical teaching. A Central Advisory Committee for the Certification of Teachers, representative of the university institutions, the training colleges, LEAs, and teachers' professional associations, would see that the standards in the groups were comparable. Officers of the Board of Education would give "active assistance" to the boards for some years.

Five of the Joint Examining Boards held their first examinations in 1929, and all eleven were in operation in 1930. Following the advice of the preparatory conferences, the Boards made few changes in the existing syllabuses. Some academic work was displaced by method courses, and larger opportunities for handicrafts were provided. Pass standards were not altered appreciably. The new procedure worked smoothly, and it was generally felt that the training colleges were using their freedom wisely. The Boards did not, however, effect the breakthrough for which many people had hoped. As will be seen, the

'McNair' Report was to criticise them severely about this. Perhaps the climate of the years militated against their success; they had to weather first the world-wide economic depression of the early 1930s, and they were hardly clear of that before the Second World War broke over their heads.

When the Board of Education accepted the Departmental Committee's recommendation that, wherever practicable, intending teachers should stay in full-time secondary education until the age of eighteen, it realised—as the Committee had done—that in many rural areas this would not be practicable, that in these areas pupil-teachership and student-teachership must continue, and that therefore special arrangements would have to be made for examining applicants for training college from such areas. Accordingly, in February 1927 the President of the Board of Education, Lord Eustace Percy, appointed a Departmental Committee to consider:

> the desirability of providing Courses of Training specially suitable for Teachers interested in country life and occupations, and the lines such courses should follow.

As the Preliminary Examination for the Certificate (by this time mainly taken by rural pupil-teachers) was to end in 1928, the President asked the Committee to consider also:

> 1 the framing of the Syllabus of an Examination which would be open to Rural Pupil-Teachers and other persons serving in country schools and which would qualify candidates either for admission to Training College or for recognition as Uncertificated Teachers;
>
> 2 the establishment of a body to conduct such an Examination.

As this was urgent the Committee dealt with it first, and in July proposed: (1) a syllabus biased towards Drawing, Gardening, Housecraft, Needlework, and Music, and (2) an approach to the Oxford and Cambridge Local Examinations Syndicate to undertake such an examination. These proposals were accepted, and the Syndicate agreed to take on the task.

Turning to its main remit, the Committee was shocked to discover that the methods employed to train pupil-teachers in rural schools were many years out of date, and that training colleges had no courses biased specifically towards teaching in rural areas. Inevitably, most college-trained teachers took posts in urban areas. In 1928 there were in the Public Elementary schools in England and Wales as a whole nearly three times as many Certificated teachers as uncertificated; but in one rural area— said to be typical—the Committee found that there were almost as many uncertificated and supplementary teachers as Certificated.

The Committee concluded that the problem of the rural areas should not be considered in isolation, but as part of a national problem; especially in view of the forthcoming reorganisation of the Public Elementary School into Primary and post-Primary units, as recommended by the Consultative Committee's Report on *The Education of the Adolescent*, which would necessarily involve also a reorganisation of teacher training.

The Committee thought that in the training of all teachers there should be a common core of academic studies, consisting of English, Geography, History, Mathematics, and Science, but that more attention should be given to Drawing, Gardening, Handicrafts, Housecraft, and Music; and, most important, that "study of the principles of education should be brought continuously to the touchstone of practical life".[7] Some training colleges should provide courses in rural studies, and there should be more supplementary courses for serving teachers, including one-year full-time courses for teachers aspiring to become heads of schools.

The Committee's Report, published in 1929, had less effect than it deserved; it was engulfed in the world-wide economic depression, which put out of court costly projects such as rural studies, and any other practical activity requiring expensive equipment.

References

1 Fisher, H A L, *An Unfinished Autobiography*, Oxford University Press, 1940, p. 91.

2 ibid., p. 92.

3 *Report of the Board of Education 1917–18*, p. 1.

4 *Report of the Departmental Committee on the Training of Teachers 1925*, Recommendations 66 and 67.

5 *Report of the Board of Education 1925–26*, p. 100.

6 *The Schoolmaster*, 22 May 1925, p. 918.

7 *Report of the Departmental Committee on the Training of Rural Teachers 1929*, p. 62.

CHAPTER SIXTEEN

Difficult Times

Hardly had the Joint Board scheme got under way before the training colleges found themselves being sucked into a morass of administrative and financial difficulties.

In July 1929 the Labour Government announced its intention to raise the school leaving age from fourteen to fifteen from 1 April 1931. Obviously, that would require many more teachers in the Elementary schools. And, with less than two years to go, those teachers must be recruited and trained as quickly as possible. Accordingly, the Board of Education asked the training colleges how many additional students they could take in the academic years 1929–30 and 1930–1.

The colleges rose magnificently to the occasion. Although their summer vacation had started, and their staffs were consequently dispersed, they managed to make arrangements to accept that autumn nearly 1,000 more students than in 1928, an increase of approximately 12 per cent. In November the Board was again on their doorsteps, asking for a larger increase in 1930–1. And again the colleges responded.

So far, so good. But when in December the President of the Board of Education, Sir Charles Trevelyan, introduced into Parliament an Education (School Attendance) Bill it ran into trouble over the question of aid from public funds to Voluntary schools. He withdrew it, and next year introduced a revised Bill. This passed a second reading in May, but got no further before the Parliamentary session ended. Meanwhile, the LEAs had made it clear that they would not give more aid to Voluntary schools unless they had more control over them. Almost in despair, Sir Charles Trevelyan introduced a third

Bill, which made no mention of financial aid. This Bill got through the Commons, but only with a crippling amendment providing that it should not come into operation until an Act had been passed authorising building grants for Voluntary schools. In February 1931 the House of Lords rejected the Bill. In March Sir Charles Trevelyan resigned.

In that month the Government, harassed by allegations that it was being extravagant, appointed a 'Committee on National Expenditure' (the 'May' Committee). The Board of Education, correctly anticipating that its income would be cut, warned the training colleges that:

> the prospects of early employment for the additional students accepted in 1929 and 1930 might not ... be ... so favourable as they would have been had the Bill become law.[1]

It suggested that colleges should leave vacancies unfilled, and accept withdrawals. But there were hardly any vacancies or withdrawals. The 1931 autumn entry exceeded that of 1928 by about 1,200.

Just as term started the Board of Education told the colleges that, domestic subjects and handicraft colleges excepted, their 1932 entry must not exceed that of 1928. A year later it told them that in 1933 they could accept only 90 per cent of the number admitted in 1932—domestic subjects and handicraft colleges again excepted. Comparable cuts were imposed upon the UTDs.

The Board realised that the cuts would cause some colleges acute financial difficulties. In consultation with the college authorities it decided that least harm would be done if a few colleges were closed. Three Church of England—Chester, Fishponds (Bristol), and Lincoln—and one LEA—Kenton (Newcastle upon Tyne)—were selected. But the proposal evoked such widespread protest that it was dropped.

The question of closures arose again in 1937. This time it was the Church of England Board of Supervision which, faithful to its policy of 'concentration', took the initiative. It recommended that three women's colleges—Brighton, Peterborough, and Truro—and one men's, Culham, should be closed. For the second time in twenty years Culham fought for its life, and for the second time successfully. It escaped because it could prove that it was financially solvent, had more applicants than places, and was acquiring a national reputation for rural science. The women's colleges, lacking so powerful a case, were closed.

By this time the reduction of student numbers had ended. The last cut, of eight per cent, was made in 1934, but no increases, except in three-year courses, were allowed in the following years. Altogether, the number of training college and UTD students had been reduced by about 20 per cent. This was not so calamitous as might at first sight appear, because the birthrate had begun to fall some years previously, and consequently the Elementary school population decreased between 1934 and 1938 by over ten per cent, from 5,712,423 to 5,510,874. There was, in fact, considerable unemployment among newly qualified teachers.

The years between the wars were years of recurrent tension for the training colleges, but it would be wrong to regard them as a period of unrelieved gloom. For some colleges they brought the realisation of long-cherished hopes. Especially, perhaps, for the Shoreditch Technical Institute, which was recognised as a training college in 1919. It achieved that status because the Board of Education, the LEAs, and the schools were recognising that "the best type of instructor in Handicraft will be one who as a Certificated teacher can take his place on the ordinary staff of the school"[2]—a belief that Shoreditch had done much to bring about. In May 1920 the Board, in Circular 1161, urged LEAs to ensure that Handicraft was taught by members of the school staff. Four months later it announced, in Circular 1177, that from January 1921 Handicraft teachers must be Certificated in order to be recognised for grant.

In May 1921 the enterprising young principal of the Loughborough Technical College, Dr Herbert Schofield, opened there a Teacher Training Department for ex-service men wishing to become Handicraft teachers. This was one of the post-war 'emergency' schemes, and like the others it closed down in 1923. But Schofield never forgot the idea; and in 1930, in conjunction with Nottingham University College, he started a two-year full-time Certificate course for teachers of art and crafts. It was to become nationally—and even internationally—famous. Six years later he began a one-year postgraduate course in physical education that was to rival it in fame.

In 1927 the Carnegie United Kingdom Trust wrote to the Association of Education Committees offering to meet the capital cost of "a national institution for the training of expert male instructors in

Physical Education".[3] After prolonged negotiations it was decided to put the institution alongside the City of Leeds Training College; and here the Carnegie College of Physical Education was opened in 1933. Unlike the women's Physical Education colleges—all still private institutions[4]—it offered no three-year courses, but only a one-year course, open to graduates and Certificated teachers.

Other specialisms were not so fortunate. The Domestic Subjects colleges were unfortunately omitted from the training 'pool' established by the Economy (Miscellaneous Provisions) Act 1926. As a result several ran into serious financial trouble, and two had to close in 1928. Happily, the AEC and other bodies pressurised the Board of Education, and in 1930 the colleges were included in the 'pool'.

The training of teachers of art and music remained less than satisfactory, though that of music teachers made some advance. In 1930 the Royal Academy of Music and the Royal College of Music introduced a joint Certificate for music teachers which carried the status of a pass degree. This was recognised by the Board of Education; but attempts to start specialist courses in training colleges had little success.

Sadly, financial difficulties ended the long and honourable career of the Home and Colonial College. Faced with the necessity of making large improvements to its premises, it could not raise sufficient money, and closed down in the summer of 1928.

References

1 *Education in 1931* (annual Report of the Board of Education), p. 47.
2 *Report of the Board of Education* 1918–19, pp. 66–67.
3 *Education*, 29 July 1927, p. 119.
4 The Chelsea College of Physical Education, being a department of the Chelsea Polytechnic, was not independent in the same sense as the other colleges. But the Polytechnics of those days were very much autonomous institutions.

CHAPTER SEVENTEEN

Freedom and Responsibility

It is dangerous to generalise about life and work in the training colleges between 1919 and 1939. The variety was very great. One trend, however, stands out. Demands from the academic staff for more freedom in the management of their professional affairs were paralleled by moves among students to get rid of authoritarian discipline and secure a responsible share in the organisation and conduct of student activities.

At Goldsmiths' College, for example, staff and students agreed that "the organisation of student life was out of date".[1] So, on student initiative, and with the blessing of the Warden, the prefect system was replaced by a Student Union modelled on university practice, and authorised to manage all student business. At the City of Leeds College a Students' Representative Council was formed in 1922, but—old conventions persisting—with separate sections for men and women. At Lincoln one of the first changes made by the principal appointed in 1924, Miss Constance Stewart, was to replace the prefect system by a College Council. On the other hand, the Darlington students' Debating Society in 1923 rejected a motion that "Self-government is advisable in Training Colleges".

Not everywhere was there sweetness and light. Even in the 1930s there were men's colleges where the students "were subjected to an iron discipline", where the register was marked at every lecture, and where there were daily roll calls;[2] and women's colleges where students were not allowed out after tea, except perhaps on Saturdays, when leave of absence might be extended to the late hour of 8 pm, or even 8.30.[3]

With the emergence of Student Unions there was a proliferation of student clubs and societies. Athletics, debating, drama, and music were the most frequent, and often the most ambitious. Leeds produced Smetana's *The Bartered Bride,* Lincoln Euripides's *Alcestis,* Sheffield Handel's *Judas Maccabaeus.* Dancing was very popular in many colleges, but not until the late 1930s did some of them dare to hold mixed dances. Segregation of the sexes persisted, too, on more formal occasions; at Sheffield, for example, until 1932 "men and women students seldom met officially even in lectures".[4]

Three main issues dominated curricula and teaching methods: (1) the perennial debate about the balance between academic and professional studies; (2) the trend, stimulated by the Hadow reports, towards 'practical' subjects in schools; and (3) the growing conviction that schooling should be 'child-centred', not subject-centred, and that therefore child study should be a principal pre-occupation of training colleges.

The academic versus professional debate brought victory to neither side. Some colleges remained strongly academic; at Westminster, for example, from 1924 "no students were admitted who were not qualified and prepared to read for the external degrees of the University of London".[5] But at Darlington the emphasis was on the college's Nursery school, and a Social Study Circle which "studied problems of housing and slum life, town planning and poverty, skilled and unskilled labour, and the adolescent in industry".[6]

The Board of Education was in general on the side of the professionals. In 1920 it reduced the number of compulsory academic subjects in the Teacher's Certificate examination from six or seven to four or five. In 1925 it allowed training colleges to give one-year courses consisting exclusively of professional studies and practice to students possessing only a Higher School Certificate. It accepted the 1925 Departmental Committee's view that training college courses should be organised primarily to produce effective teachers. It repeatedly emphasised the importance of the 'practical' subjects, especially in 1929 and 1930 when it was expected that the school leaving age would be raised. It campaigned, with much success, for better teaching of physical education in schools and training colleges.

The most important change in the training colleges during these twenty years was the shift in educational values. "What *was* established firmly during the period between the World Wars," wrote Professor John Tibble in 1963, "was the central place of child study in the college education courses."[7] What was *not* established, unfortunately, was the brand of educational psychology best fitted to underpin this study. Behaviourism, *Gesalt*, and psychoanalysis jostled each other for the favours of staff and students. "The effect in the training world of this ferment of opposing schools of thought in psychology," said Tibble, "was to produce an atmosphere of uncertainty and confusion with regard to the content of the education course." What was more serious was that much of the psychology taught was felt by students (and HMI) to have little relevance to what happened in school classrooms.

It must not be thought from this that all, or most, of the training was irrelevant. Much of it was very much to the point, partly because of the increased emphasis upon teaching practice in realistic conditions. More time was allocated to practice, and more reality injected into it by the use of a wide range of ordinary schools instead of the highly artificial 'Demonstration' or 'Practising' school attached to, and at least partly staffed by, a training college. Not altogether unconnected with this change was the general abandonment of the traditional titles of 'Master' and 'Mistress' of Method in favour of the more appropriate (and more modest) title of 'Lecturer in Education'. Also connected was the gradual disuse—to the enormous relief of thousands of students—of the age-old 'Criticism' lesson.

The Joint Boards made no large changes in examining techniques or standards. Theoretical studies continued to be generally assessed by written papers marked numerically. Practical teaching, still assessed by HMI, was graded on a five-point scale, and the student's 'general suitability' for teaching was recorded in a confidential report from the college to the employing LEA or school managers.

The most significant changes in the UTDs were the rapid discarding in the early 1920s of their two-year courses for Elementary school teachers, and the more gradual squeezing-out of three-year students. The pace of these processes varied in individual cases, but by 1925 few non-graduates were being trained in UTDs. Most of the students were concluding a four-year course taken throughout at the same university, but a few had graduated elsewhere. Taking advantage of a concession made in the Board of Education's 1922 Regulations, one university after another substituted an 'Alternative Examination' for a Diploma in place of the Teacher's Certificate examination, and by the 1930s this had become the general practice.

References

1 Dymond, op. cit. p. 115.
2 *The Times Educational Supplement,* 10 October 1969, article by J Pashley entitled "Those dear old golden rule days".
3 *The Training of Teachers,* A Memorandum drawn up by the Joint Standing Committee of the Training College Association and the Council of Principals, University of London Press, 1939, p. 38.
4 Millington, Roy, op. cit. p. 73.
5 Pritchard, F C, op. cit. p. 138.
6 Stanton, O M, op. cit. p. 145.
7 *The Year Book of Education 1963:* The Education and Training of Teachers, edited by Bereday, G Z F, and Lauwerys, J A. Evans Brothers in association with the University of London Institute of Education, and Teachers College, Columbia University, New York, 1963, p. 92.

CHAPTER EIGHTEEN

The McNair Report

The Second World War, like the first, hit the men's training colleges hard, though not so severely; by 1942–43, the worst year, the number of their students was under one-quarter of the 1938–9 figure. The UTDs were again decimated; from 1941 to 1944 they contained under 60 men—as against 970 in 1938–39. Women were, as in 1914–18, urged to regard teaching as national service; and they responded so well that the number in training (except in DS colleges) never fell more than marginally below the pre-war level, and by 1943–44 was beginning to exceed it.

Many colleges were evacuated, some because they were in potentially dangerous areas, others because their premises were requisitioned. A few had to migrate more than once; one or two, like Westminster, had their students distributed in several institutions. Others, including the recurrently unfortunate Culham, were 'temporarily' closed. Much more material damage was done to college buildings by enemy action than during the First World War.

Planning for post-war reform began as early as 1941. In that year the Board of Education sent to a large number of organisations the famous 'Green Book'—so called from the colour of its cover—a comprehensive analysis of the English educational system, and suggestions for its reform. It noted:

> The need to review the methods of recruiting to and training for the teaching profession, especially in the light of any decisions that may be taken as to the general framework of post-war education.

In March 1942 the President of the Board of Education, Mr R A (later Lord) Butler, appointed a committee of ten persons under the chairmanship of the Vice-Chancellor of Liverpool University, Sir Arnold McNair, to investigate:

> the present sources of supply and the methods of recruitment and training of teachers and youth leaders and to report what principles should guide the Board in these matters in the future.

The 'McNair' Report was published in May 1944, three months before the Education Act received the Royal Assent. It dealt comprehensively with the recognition, supply, and training of teachers for Primary and Secondary schools and Further Education colleges, and of leaders for the Service of Youth. In doing so, it took into consideration the reforms in the educational system which appeared to have been generally agreed, including the raising of the school leaving age, expansion of nursery education, reduction in the size of classes, the ranking of all forms of post-primary schooling as Secondary, and the introduction of compulsory part-time education beyond the school leaving age.

In the following pages attention is concentrated upon the committee's recommendations for the training of teachers, but it should not be overlooked that it made equally important recommendations about the other matters in its terms of refernece. They included:

1 A basic salary scale for all qualified teachers.

2 Recognition by the Board of Education of only one grade of teacher, the 'Qualified Teacher'.

3 This status to be accorded to persons who have "satisfactorily completed an approved course of education and training", and, at the discretion of the Board, to "persons with good academic or other attainments".

4 Abolition of the 'Pledge'.[1]

The committee condemned "existing arrangements for the recognition, the training and the supply of teachers" as "chaotic and ill-adjusted even to present needs".[2] Most colleges were too small; many were poorly housed and equipped. A two-year course for non-graduates was too short; "many students ... do not mature by living; they survive by hurrying".[3] The fundamental weakness of the system was that the 100 institutions engaged in teacher training were "not related to one another in such a way as to produce a coherent training service".[4]

Unfortunately, on the vital issue of how to administer such a service the committee split. Five members, including the chairman, wanted enlarged Joint Boards to do it. The other five felt that only "a major constitutional change ... in the organisation and administration of the education and training of teachers"[5] would suffice. Both groups wanted the service to be locally administered by universities and training colleges working in co-operation. But they differed fundamentally about the nature of that co-operation. The chairman's group wanted "a partnership between equals"; they did not want the universities to be *responsible* for the training of teachers. But that was precisely what the other group did want.

> We do not believe that any area system for the training of teachers can be effective unless those who shoulder the responsibility derive their authority from a source which, because of its recognised standards and its standing in the educational world, commands the respect of all the partners concerned and which, because of its established independence, is powerful enough to resist the encroachments of centralisation.[6]

"The universities," declared this group, "embody these standards and have this standing and this independence." The group proposed that each university should establish a School of Education, which it defined as "an organised federation of approved training institutions working in co-operation with other approved educational institutions". The School would be responsible for the training and assessment of all students in its area who were seeking recognition as Qualified Teachers.[7]

Ultimate control of the School would lie with the university, immediate control with a Delegacy consisting primarily of representatives of the university and the training institutions. The School's premises would be supplied and owned by the university. The training institutions would retain their governing bodies, and would select their students; but the appointment of principals and senior members of staff would require the approval of the Delegacy.

After the publication of the Report there followed a period of inconclusive discussion. Neither 'Scheme A', as the School of

Education plan came to be known, nor 'Scheme B', the Joint Board proposal, could command sufficient support to carry the day. Nor could a suggested 'Scheme C', in which an area training organisation not headed by a university would be financed by direct grant from the Ministry of Education. In June 1946 the Minister, Miss Ellen Wilkinson, tiring of the delay, told the universities that:

> provided in each case the co-operation of the individual training colleges and local education authorities was secured, some diversity of organisation would be accepted.[8]

Ultimately, most universities agreed to establish a modified form of 'Scheme A'. This retained the idea of a "federation of approved training institutions" headed by the university, but dropped that of a School of Education in favour of an area training organisation (ATO) serviced by an Institute of Education staffed and housed by the university. An important difference between the two schemes was that in the one adopted the University Training Department was not wholly absorbed into the ATO; while participating in its activities it remained a separate university department.[9]

Several ATOs began work in 1947, and although the establishment of one or two was delayed, all were in operation by 1951. For thirteen of the sixteen established in England, and the one in Wales, responsibility had been accepted by a university or university college. The three non-university ATOs were at Cambridge, Liverpool, and Reading. Later, Liverpool and Reading Universities were to accept responsibility.

References

1 *Teachers and Youth Leaders* (the 'McNair' Report), pp. 44 and 45.
2 ibid., p. 18.
3 ibid., p. 65. This well-known comment was coined by Mr S H Wood, head of the Teachers Branch of the Board of Education, who had been made a full member of the Committee, and who drafted much of its Report.
4 ibid., pp. 48–49.
5 ibid., p. 48.
6 ibid., p. 50.
7 ibid., p. 54.
8 Circular 112, *Organisation of the Training of Teachers*, dated 11 June 1946.

9 The Universities of Manchester and Wales established Schools of Education, for different reasons, and of different forms.

CHAPTER NINETEEN

Area Training Organisation

Though the establishment of ATOs was spread over five years (1947–51), fourteen of the seventeen original ones (more followed later) had been constituted and were at work by the end of 1948.[1] All but one of these were university ATOs. The single exception, Reading, was a body established by a Declaration of Trust. It was financed by direct grant from the Ministry of Education, and governed by a Board on which sat representatives of the university, the training colleges, and the LEAs in its area. Similar ATOs were constituted at Cambridge and Liverpool in 1949, but the latter was short-lived; the university took over in 1954. A year later, Reading University also assumed responsibility.

The term 'Area Training Organisation', though it continued to be used in Ministerial documents, was in common parlance soon replaced by 'Institute of Education' ('School' in the case of Manchester and Wales), though strictly speaking 'Institute' applied only to the salaried staff employed to service the ATO, or the premises in which they worked.

The ATOs varied greatly in size, and in the number of their member institutions. London was not the largest in geographical area, but otherwise was much the biggest; at its inception it contained 38 colleges and departments, and nearly 7,000 students. At the opposite extreme the University College of the South West (Exeter), though it covered a huge area, mainly rural, included only two colleges and one UTD. Intermediately, six ATOs had ten or eleven colleges each, containing between 1,400 and 2,000 students. In every ATO there was at least one UTD; Durham, London, and Manchester had two each, and Wales four.

The Universities of London and Wales had particular difficulties to overcome in constituting ATOs. London already had an Institute of Education, but one with very different functions from those proposed for an ATO; it was, in fact, a large and many-faceted University Department of Education, which had developed a very wide range of courses, and had attracted numerous students from oversea countries. It had high prestige in the University, and this its director, Dr. G B Jeffery, was determined to preserve. So, when he planned the constitution of the new Institute, he was careful to give the old one a central, and semi-autonomous, position in it.

Wales's problem was a territorial one. It had four University Colleges, two of which, Aberystwyth and Bangor, were distant from the other two, Cardiff and Swansea, and linked with them, and with each other, only by awkwardly indirect routes. The problem was solved by establishing more or less independent Faculties of Education in the colleges, and co-ordinating their activities by means of a secretariat located at Cardiff.

The administrative structures of the other Institutes were basically similar, though the names of their constituent parts varied. Some Institutes called their governing body a Delegacy, others a Board; in all cases, however, this consisted of representatives of the university, the Institute, the training colleges, and the LEAs in the Institute area, with representatives of the Ministry of Education and HM Inspectorate attending as assessors. Regrettably, representatives of the teaching profession were not usually invited during the early years, even as co-opted members.

The governing bodies of all university ATOs had to report to Senate, which had the power to approve, reject, amend, or refer back any of their recommendations. The point is important. Many people assumed that Institutes of Education were independent bodies; they were not. They could always be over-ridden by their universities, which could even close them.

Most Institutes were headed by Directors, most of whom had, or were accorded, professional status. Seven universities, including London, appointed the professor who was in charge of the UTD (or UDE, as education departments were beginning to be styled). In Wales the four professional heads of the college UDEs were made heads of the Faculties of Education.

According to the Ministry of Education, every ATO had five basic functions.

1 Supervise the courses of training in member colleges, and further their work in every possible way.

2 Recommend to the Minister of Education for the status of Qualified Teacher students who had successfully completed courses of training in member colleges or departments of education.

3 Plan the development of training facilities in their area.

4 Provide an education centre for students in training, serving teachers in the area, and other persons interested in education.

5 Provide facilities for further study and research, including refresher and other short courses for serving teachers.[2]

On this common foundation Institutes soon began to build particular strengths, usually in one of three areas: research, teaching, and extra-mural activities. Birmingham was pre-eminently a research Institute, for reasons easy to explain. From 1919 to 1946 the head of the UDE was Professor C W Valentine, who during those years achieved an international reputation in the field of educational research. When, in 1947, the University established its Institute of Education, it appointed two professors: M V C Jeffreys as director of the Institute, and F J (later Sir Fred) Schonell, who was already well known for his researches, as head of the UDE. A joint department of of Research was formed, and staffed by members from both the Institute and the UDE, together with some specially appointed Research Fellows. In the year 1948–9 a Remedial Centre was added. It had three main functions: (1) to do original research, (2) to provide a training ground for students in the University departments of education, psychology, paediatrics and child health, and in the member training colleges, and (3) to assist the LEAs in the Institute area by investigating and treating educational retardation among children of normal and above-normal intelligence. So successful was the Centre that within ten years it had become a Department of Child Study; because, as the Institute's Report for 1957–8 commented: "Over the years the scope of the research and clinical work has broadened beyond the confines of remedial education."

Leeds quickly became a teaching Institute. Established in 1948, during its first year it provided, in co-operation with LEAs, thirty-five short courses for teachers. In the next year it added one-year full-time and two-year part-time courses leading to Diplomas; by 1950 it was running three of these, in Primary Education, Religious Education, and Educational Administration, and was preparing one in Secondary Education. Full-time lecturers were appointed to the Institute staff to take charge of these courses, but most of the teaching was done by members of the staffs of the University, training colleges, schools, or education offices. In 1955 the director of the Institute, Professor W R Niblett, could claim that sixty members of the University staff, from twenty-seven departments, were teaching in Institute Diploma courses, and as many, if not more, in its shorter courses.

Southampton was an example of an 'extra-mural' Institute. From the start it concentrated on short courses and conferences for serving teachers. In its first annual Report (1950–1) it claimed that there was already emerging a pattern in its programme.

> ... the straight lecture-course, with discussions ... the two-day course of a more concentrated kind, which meets the needs of teachers in scattered areas ... the one-day conference which ... makes it possible to combine ... a meeting with a visit to an exhibition ... [and] the conference designed as a starting point for further development.

In the following year about 1,400 people participated in Institute courses, conferences, and discussion groups. (Some of these took place in the Channel Islands, which the Institute had accepted into its area.) By 1954–5 the number had risen to over 7,000.

Whatever their special interests, nearly all the Institutes got off to a good start, despite in many cases cramped accommodation and not enough staff. The latter shortage for long hampered a development which would certainly have been valuable, and which many people felt to be essential; the provision of local centres, especially in ATO areas containing much rural country. Institutes tried various means to meet this deficiency. Exeter, whose area covered Devon, Cornwall, and the Scilly Isles, appointed a resident tutor in Cornwall. Other Institutes bought or hired buses. But no expedient completely solved the problem. An unfortunate consequence was that for years some

Institutes were little more than a name to teachers in outlying districts.

To enable ATOs "to concert policy where this is desirable, and in particular to ensure a common policy in recommending students for the status of qualified teacher, while still permitting the greatest possible variety in courses", the Minister established in 1948 a Standing Conference of Area Training Organisations (SCATO).[3] A responsible brief, but SCATO was not very effective for very long. It began briskly, but was soon restricted to meeting once a year, for the exchange of views, and in 1958 to meeting only when a constituent member felt this necessary. By then the Directors of the Institutes and Schools of Education had formed their own association, which they nicknamed—half seriously—the 'CID' (Conference of Institute Directors). Meeting at first quite informally (and with no holds barred!), it soon attracted the attention of the senior Civil Servants in the Ministry, and before long had two meetings every time it assembled in London; one on its own, and one with the top brass of the Teacher Training Branch. There was never any lack of matters to discuss; the CID became a sounding board for Ministry ideas—and a ruthless wrecker of the less practicable. It was an interesting example of influence without power. As salaried employees, the directors had no power to commit their employers to any policy or action. But the influence they exerted through the CID was, at any rate for some years, very considerable.[4]

References

1 Four Institutes were established in 1947, by the Universities of Birmingham and Bristol, and the University Colleges of Nottingham and Southampton. Ten followed in 1948, at Durham, Exeter, Hull, Leeds, Leicester, London, Manchester, Reading (non-university), Sheffield, and in Wales.

2 *Education in 1948*, pp. 55–6.

3 ibid., p. 57.

4 In 1967 the CID amalgamated with the Conference of Heads of University Departments of Education (CHUDE) to form the University Council for the Education of Teachers (UCET).

CHAPTER TWENTY

"Into the Breach"

By mid-1943 it seemed practically certain that when the war was over the school-leaving age would be raised from fourteen to fifteen. That would mean ... well, no one quite knew how many additional teachers it would mean, but 50,000 was a popular estimate. That was why the Emergency Scheme for the Recruitment and Training of Teachers was devised.

The idea was not new; as has been recorded in Chapter 14, several small emergency training schemes were carried out during and after the First World War. It seems clear that by 1943 officers at the Board of Education had had a good look at these. During the summer the Deputy Secretary, Mr R S (later Sir Robert) Wood, and the Head of the Teacher Training Branch, Mr S H Wood, toured the country to sound opinion among teachers and administrators about mounting an emergency scheme. The arguments they used in favour were: (1) during the years immediately following the war at least 50,000 new teachers would be wanted; (2) the existing training facilities were quite inadequate to meet such a demand; (3) men and women in HM Forces were wishing to be trained; and (4) the nation could not afford to let slip anyone who seemed likely to make a good teacher.

There was considerable opposition from teachers to the suggestion that the training course should last only one year. The cry of 'Dilution!' resounded. Nevertheless, most people realised that some exceptional action must be taken, and many felt that such an emergency scheme as was proposed might well attract men and women of good quality.

In October 1943 the NUT published its views in a pamphlet entitled *Recruitment and Supply of Teachers: A Short Term Policy for an*

Emergency. The Union said that without special measures it would be impossible even to maintain the existing strength of the teaching force in the schools, let alone provide for "a 50 per cent increase on the present establishment of 170,000". It accepted the idea of an emergency training scheme, and made the following proposals: (1) the minimum academic qualification for entry should be a School Certificate, or an equivalent; (2) accepted candidates should do at least a month in school to test their aptitude for teaching; (3) their training should be for at least twelve months, and should be followed by directed study for three to four years culminating in a term at least in a training college; and (4) though paid as Certificated Teachers, they should not be fully recognised until they had completed this refresher course in college.

The scheme was perhaps too elaborate, but it had valuable points, some of which were incorporated in the Emergency scheme that was finally adopted. In December 1943 the President of the Board of Education, Mr R A Butler, appointed a committee representative of the Board, the LEAs, and the teachers' associations, under the chairmanship of Mr G N (later Sir Gilbert) Flemming, then an Assistant Secretary at the Board, to study the problems of emergency training, and outline a scheme. In May 1944 the committee's proposed scheme appeared as an appendix to Circular 1652, *Emergency Recruitment and Training of Teachers.* Its principal points were:

1 Men and women between approximately the ages of 21 and 35 who had served in HM Forces or other forms of national service for at least twelve months during the war should be invited to apply for a one-year course of training, followed by two years of part-time study while teaching. On the successful completion of training and study they would receive the Teacher's Certificate, and be granted the status of Qualified Teacher.

2 Candidates would be admitted to the course on the basis of careful individual selection. They would have to show that they were capable of profiting from the training, and would be likely to become effective teachers. But selection would not be restricted to those who possessed some specific academic qualification.

3 The course should consist mainly of professional training, but

every student should be required to take a course in the use of
the English language, and to study one or more subjects of
general education for his/her personal development.

4 Colleges for emergency training should have a substantial
nucleus of full-time staff, but should make the fullest use also of
part-time and visiting staff, not all of whom need necessarily be
professional teachers.

5 Students' work would be assessed, not by formal external
examinations, but by internal tests subject to external checks.

6 The period of probation for emergency-trained teachers should
be two years. During this time they should follow courses of part-
time study related to their previous attainments, their aptitudes,
and the opportunities open to them.

The most crucial sentences in the report were:

We do not regard the students to be trained under the
Emergency Scheme as mere stop-gaps who are to be rushed into
the schools to tide over an immediate crisis. If the scheme is
justified at all, they must like other students be regarded as
potential teachers in the fullest sense, who ... when they receive
their full recognition, take their place as equals beside teachers
who have entered the profession through other and more usual
channels.

Everyone concerned realised that the Emergency Scheme involved
risks. To get some idea of the problems that might arise a pilot scheme
was undertaken in 1944–5 by the Goldsmiths' College training
department, then evacuated to Nottingham University College.
Twenty-seven men and one woman, all discharged from HM Forces
for medical reasons, were selected as students. The course comprised
four elements: Professional Studies, Language and Number,
'Particular Studies', and Teaching Practice. Particular Studies meant
one Main and one or two Subsidiary subjects, to be chosen from a list
of nine ordinarily taught in training colleges. A relatively large
amount of time was allotted to teaching practice: fourteen weeks,
made up of two weeks in the first term, four in the second, and two
periods of four weeks in the third. In addition, students spent
approximately half a day a week observing in schools.

The main conclusions reached were: (1) careful selection of students, with particular attention to personal quality, was most important; (2) most students should attempt only one Main and one Subsidiary subject; (3) professional studies, especially psychology, should be related as closely as possible to work seen in schools; (4) the amount of time given to teaching practice was not excessive; and (5) continuous assessment throughout the course was practicable, and preferable to a formal final examination.

Recruitment for the Emergency Scheme began in December 1944, but was limited to: (1) ex-Servicemen and women discharged on medical grounds; (2) men graded physically unfit for active service; and (3) women in civilian occupations ranked as war service. Even so, 7,000 applications were received within three months. In June 1945—shortly after the end of the war in Europe—the Scheme was opened to all men and women who had served for a year or more in HM Forces or a war industry. Applications poured in; by December they were averaging 5,000 a month, and swamping the selection panels. Soon, two ever-lengthening waiting lists built up: of applicants for interview, and accepted candidates for whom there were not as yet places in college. The latter was the more serious, because it consisted of people approved as fit for training; but finding and adapting premises for colleges was proving unexpectedly difficult. By December 1945 only six colleges, accommodating just over 1,000 students, had been opened—but there were more than 5,000 accepted candidates, 15,000 applicants awaiting interview, and "fresh applications coming in at the rate of over 1,000 a week".[1]

Recriminations filled the air. But slowly—too slowly, it seemed at the time—more colleges were opened. By December 1946 there were 31, with 7,350 places, by December 1947, fifty-five (the total number opened), offering nearly 13,500 places. By then the waiting lists had shrunk to manageable size, largely because the recruitment of men had ceased in the previous June. But also because over 7,500 applications had been withdrawn.

The first three colleges, opened in May 1945, were Wall Hall, near Watford, Exhall, near Coventry, and Alnwick Castle, in Northumberland. Their buildings were typical of the variegated assortment that was to be used: a large country house, a hutted hostel for wartime factory workers, and a baronial castle. Later acquisitions included hotels and boarding houses, disused colleges and schools, office blocks, hospitals—and an establishment for destitute men.

The students were of all ages from twenty-one to over fifty. They came from a wide range of civilian occupations, though clerical workers predominated. Over three-quarters had had some Secondary or Technical education, and about half had a School Certificate or higher qualification. Of those enrolled during the earlier years of the Scheme it was said that, "Three characteristics stood out: their keenness and singleness of purpose; the wide range of their talents and accomplishments; and their powers of initiative and organisation."[2]

Much the same can be said of the staff. Many had served in HM Forces; at Didsbury College, for example, three-quarters of them. "The fact that we had come straight from the job," wrote one teacher many years later, "gave us an overwhelming pull over the normal training college lecturer. But," he added, "even this fact cut no ice with ex-forces types—who were quick to detect and denounce the least sign of waffle, flannel, or bull."[3]

Staff were recruited from every branch of the teaching profession, but nearly three-quarters came from Secondary schools. Only 14 per cent came from Primary schools, and under five per cent from training colleges. A small number came from Further Education, chiefly to man the three colleges reserved in 1945 for the training of teachers of technical subjects.

Whatever their origin, they were during the earlier years as enthusiastic as the students. And they worked equally hard. They had to; apart from the exigencies of an over-exacting timetable, they had to deal with students who:

> have been described as arriving in college in the state of mind as of one hurrying for a train, and anything which appeared to stay or deflect their progress towards becoming efficient practical teachers in the shortest possible time was regarded with something more than impatience.[4]

The course was originally planned to occupy 52 weeks, of which 48 were to be spent in study and teaching practice, and four on vacation—two periods of one week each and one of a fortnight. That arrangement did not last very long; the pace was too hot. Staff and students alike wilted under the strain. In January 1946 the four weeks of vacation were doubled, and staffs were given up to seven weeks between courses for rest and forward planning. These relaxations probably prevented a serious lowering of standards, if not the breakdown of the scheme.

A major problem that persisted throughout was the difficulty many students had in acquiring, or recovering, the habit of systematic study. It showed itself most clearly in failure to use to good advantage the generous amount of time allotted to private study. Over-conscientious students—and there were many of them—either spent such long hours in 'free' study that they came to their classes too tired to profit; or, finding they could not work well on their own, began to worry and grow depressed.

Many staff found teaching practice a formidable business. Frequently, their allotted areas would be already 'saturated' with students from permanent training colleges.[5] In some cases they had to send students to their home towns, in others to put them into lodgings far from the college. The size of the Scheme necessitated using some 3,000 schools which had never taken students before, and so it was often a case of students who had never taught being supervised by tutors with little or no experience of supervision, in schools with little or no experience of having students. Happily, in most cases all concerned seem to have made a reasonably good job of it.

The Emergency Scheme was designed to train many more men than women. But by 1947 it had become clear that (1) more men had returned to teaching from war service than had been expected, and (2) because of the rising birth-rate, more women teachers of young children were urgently needed. So from June 1947 recruitment of men ceased, while a publicity campaign was launched to attract women. Several Emergency colleges for men were made co-educational; and during 1948 and 1949 fourteen men's or co-educational Emergency colleges became permanent women's colleges. This operation was not, unfortunately, carried out as humanely as could have been wished, many staff being left much too long in doubt about the future of their college and their jobs.

The transformation of Emergency into permanent colleges began the run-down of the Emergency Training Scheme. By December 1949 the number of Emergency colleges had fallen from 55 to 33. In August 1951 the last college, at Wandsworth in west London, was closed; in December, at Trent Park in Middlesex, the last group of emergency-trained teachers finished their course.

The least satisfactory part of the Emergency Training Scheme was the two-year probationary period. In May 1946 the Minister of Education, Miss Ellen Wilkinson, in Circular 106, appealed to the LEAs for help. The response was extremely varied; some LEAs did much, some little, some nothing. Positive responses ranged from appointing a retired teacher to look after the probationers to the arrangement of regional schemes covering the areas of several LEAs. But the problem was nowhere completely solved, if only because, as one emergency-trained teacher commented, "The trouble with part-time study is that there is no part-time."[6] The excuse was valid from men and women settling simultaneously into civilian life and a new profession.

For many years teachers and administrators debated the value of the Emergency Scheme. What is certain is that it produced about 35,000 Qualified Teachers, and thus made practicable the raising of the school leaving age in 1947. (By 1951 one in six of the teachers in maintained schools was emergency-trained.) Many of them proved above-average teachers, and more than a few first-class. On the other hand, there was possibly a higher proportion of weak teachers than among those produced by permanent training colleges.

The permanent colleges benefited from the recruitment of staff with experience of the Emergency Scheme. A large number of schools benefited from having had:

> their day-to-day routine enlivened, and their teaching methods in some degree enriched by the freshness of approach of keen students, and ... intercourse with college tutors who were themselves actively re-sorting their habits of thinking.[7]

A very valuable pendant to the Emergency Scheme was the wholesale training of uncertificated teachers. In 1946 the Minister of Education, Miss Ellen Wilkinson, announced that it was the Government's policy to have only Qualified Teachers, maintained schools, and that she was therefore offering courses leading to the Teacher's Certificate to all uncertificated teachers in these schools who had between five and fifteen years' service. (Teachers with more than fifteen would, given a satisfactory report on their work, be granted the Certificate on the grounds of long service; those with less than five must take a normal two-year course.)

About half of the 7,000 uncertificated teachers in maintained schools were eligible for the one-year course. There were 1,944 applicants (131 men, 1,863 women) for the first course, held in 1947–8; of these 444 (58 men, 386 women) were selected, preference being given to those with the longest service. Further courses were held in 1948–9 and 1949–50, and smaller groups were trained between 1950 and 1952; altogether about 2,200 teachers secured Certificates by these means. Some 500 younger teachers took two-year courses. By 1953 the number of uncertificated teachers in maintained schools was under 2,000.

Thanks to the principal of Exhall College, Miss Helen Simpson, I had the unique experience of spending two days there, during a course for uncertificated teachers, one shortly after it began, and the other towards its close. The difference was amazing: a near-miraculous transformation. The uncertificated teachers had come in diffident, resentful, suspicious. They went out self-confident and serene. One said to me: "Now we'll really show them!"

References

1 *Challenge and Response*: An Account of the Emergency Scheme for the Training of Teachers, Ministry of Education Pamphlet No. 17, HMSO, 1950, p. 11.
2 ibid., p. 36.
3 *The Teacher*, 24 September 1965, article entitled "Operation Bypass", by A M Robertson.
4 *Challenge and Response*, pp. 57–58.
5 A district was said to be 'saturated' when six out of ten of its schools had students on teaching practice.
6 *Challenge and Response*, p. 119.
7 ibid., p. 63.

CHAPTER TWENTY ONE

Massive Expansion

Alongside the Emergency Scheme went expansion of the permanent training institutions. In February 1945 the Minister issued Regulations sanctioning the payment, in aid of a Voluntary college or hostel, of grants not exceeding one-half of any approved expenditure incurred on the improvement, extension, or replacement of existing accommodation, and on any furniture or equipment which this necessitated. Grant would be paid, however, in respect of established colleges only; it was not available for the founding of new colleges. In April 1946, in order to ensure that no suitable applicant to a Voluntary college would be prevented from entering by lack of means, the Minister ended the system of fixed *per capita* grants, and undertook to pay students' tuition fees, and boarding fees less the 'student's contribution'.[1]

The 1945 Regulations were intended to discourage the founding of Voluntary colleges; new colleges were to be provided by LEAs. In July 1946 the Minister offered the LEAs 100 per cent grant on the establishment, equipment, and maintenance of training colleges and hostels.[2] Forty per cent of the grant would come from the LEAs themselves, for all would contribute to a 'pool' an annual sum based on the number of children attending maintained schools in their areas. On the total amount contributed the Minister would pay the normal grant, then about 60 per cent.

This offer quickly produced impressive results. Nine new LEA colleges were opened in 1946–7, and ten in 1947–8. Because of shortage of building labour and materials, none started in new premises. (Those opened in 1948 were Emergency colleges made permanent.) The new policy altered drastically within a few years the relative contributions to the training of teachers of statutory and voluntary organisations. In 1939 there were 63 Voluntary and 28 LEA colleges; by 1951 there were 76 LEA and 56 Voluntary. The only Voluntary body to increase the number of its colleges during this period was the Roman Catholic Church: from 9 to 13.

By 1951 there were nearly 25,000 students in training, more than twice as many as in 1939. Even this large increase was insufficient to keep pace with the needs of the schools. As new building was next to impossible, in 1946 the Minister asked the colleges to overcrowd their accommodation; and except between 1950 and 1955 overcrowding was to be the rule for many years. The reason why the pressure relaxed from 1950 to 1955 was a sudden (and unexpected) shortage of applicants for training. The stream of entrants from HM Forces and war industries dried up, and it was discovered that too few boys and girls were staying long enough at school to secure the required entry qualifications. Girls were in particularly short supply, despite the fact that the training colleges were getting 60 per cent of all girls who stayed at school until seventeen and did not go on to university. In the early 1950s several women's colleges could not fill all their places.

Clearly, unless new sources of supply were found, the schools would be seriously understaffed. Various remedies were suggested: recruitment from Secondary Modern schools on the basis of personal rather than academic qualifications, revival of the pupil-teacher system, employment of unqualified assistants to Qualified Teachers. The teachers' associations opposed all such proposals; only applicants with the required academic qualifications—from 1951, when the General Certificate of Education (GCE) was introduced, a minimum of five Ordinary level passes—should be allowed to enter training college, and only Qualified Teachers to serve in the schools.

In 1954 a report made by the Central Advisory Council on Education (England) on *Early Leaving* pointed to an obvious remedy.

> In English Grammar schools in 1953 about 10,000 boys and 7,000 girls completed advanced courses, i.e. GCE 'A' level courses ... about 5,000 more boys and 5,000 more girls could very well have done so if they had stayed longer at school.[3] -

Despite the shortfall in applicants, and a warning from the recently established National Advisory Council on the Training and Supply of Teachers (NACTST)[4] that even if every place in the colleges and

UDEs was filled every year the output of trained teachers would not even maintain existing staffing ratios, in 1951 the Minister risked a further decrease in supply by abolishing the 'Pledge', the scheme whereby UDE applicants contracted to teach for a specified number of years in maintained schools in return for grants carrying them through a four-year university course. Henceforth, they would merely have to sign a 'Declaration of Intent' to teach in maintained schools.

Few people regretted the passing of the Pledge. When it was introduced, in 1911, it offered to poor boys and girls the only large-scale opportunity to go to university. Forty years later State scholarships and LEA grants had transformed the situation—which is not to say that this was entirely satisfactory. The Minister recognised that it needed improving, and doubled the number of State scholarships awarded annually (from 900 to 1,850); and at the same time offered to supplement more Open scholarships if the universities could provide more without lowering academic standards.

The result of abolishing the Pledge was that the number of entrants into UDEs fell for three years. Then it started rising again, and by 1960 was increasing in almost exact proportion to the increase in the total number of university entrants. Set against the needs of the schools, this was not fast enough, but fortunately the training colleges were doing much better. By 1960 their annual intake was more than twice as large as in 1947: 14,844, as against 7,090.

In September 1960 the two-year training college course was lengthened to three years. Many Jeremiahs had prophesied that when the college course became as long as an undergraduate course, the number of applicants to the colleges would fall. They were proved resoundingly wrong; the 1960 figure was almost 1,000 up on that of 1959, and subsequent years also showed increases. The 1960s were, in fact, the years of largest growth.

A difficult problem was how to produce in the right proportions the different kinds of teachers required. In October 1960 the Minister, in Training College Letter 14/60, ruled that 85 per cent of students in training colleges must be trained for Primary school service, and the other 15 per cent for 'shortage' subjects in Secondary schools. The colleges protested strongly against this so-called 'Balance of Training'; it meant in effect, they said, that training colleges were to train Primary school teachers, UDEs Secondary: a divisive and retrograde state of affairs. They had to submit; but it was rare to find a college training anything like 85 per cent of its students exclusively for Primary work. The compromise usually adopted was to organise a 'Junior-Secondary' course covering work in upper Junior and lower Secondary classes. This was not infrequently the largest course in a college.

Various other measures were taken to produce more teachers for 'shortage' subjects. Emergency colleges turned permanent specialised in these subjects. Five of the independent colleges training women teachers of physical education became LEA colleges, and thus enabled to expand. The West Riding of Yorkshire added a sixth by founding Lady Mabel College at Wentworth near Rotherham. Attempts were made to attract more serving teachers into Supplementary courses, but these had little success until 1955, when secondment on full salary replaced the inadequate grants previously offered.

No account of the training of teachers during the first fifteen or twenty years after the 1939–45 war can ignore the huge proliferation of short courses for serving teachers. It covered every aspect of the theory and practice of education, and every subject in the school curriculum. The courses ranged in quality from excellent to almost valueless. Too many were pedestrian, platitudinous, or non-participatory—all lecture and no discussion—and some, alas! manifested all these faults. But many, perhaps most, were conscientious and helpful attempts to assist teachers in their "daily round and common task", and as such were enormously appreciated, especially by those who had never had such assistance before.

During the war the provision of short courses had practically ceased. In 1945 the Ministry organised a modest programme on the pre-war pattern. Most of the courses were over-subscribed. In 1946 it arranged many more courses, and again most were over-subscribed. Not until 1951 did supply meet demand, and then only because of the large number of courses provided by LEAs, Institutes of Education, and teachers' associations.

The Ministry's courses covered most subjects taught in Primary and Secondary schools, the education of handicapped children, school meals, the Youth Service, and Adult Education. Courses held in Europe were (not surprisingly) extremely popular; in 1947 one in Paris for teachers of French attracted 700 applicants for 100 places.

In the earlier years the Ministry provided local, regional, national, and international courses; from 1951 it concentrated on the national and international, leaving the local and regional increasingly to the LEAs, Institutes of Education, teachers' organisations and other voluntary bodies.

A particularly interesting instance of an international course was the one held at Bangor in North Wales in 1952, when 170 teachers of English as a foreign language, drawn from 20 countries, assembled under the auspices of the Welsh Department of the Ministry of Education. Among the bodies sponsoring members were the War Office, the Colonial Office, the British Council, the Committee for the Education of Poles in England, and private industry.

References

1 *The Training of Teachers Grant Regulations 1946*, dated 29 April 1946, Reg. 22. The 'student's contribution' was the amount due from his/her parents (or the student if independent of them). It was based on a net income scale drawn up by the Ministry of Education.

2 *The Local Education Authorities Grant Regulations 1946*, dated 23 July 1946, Sections 9 and 10.

3 *Early Leaving*: A Report of the Central Advisory Council for Education (England), HMSO, 1954, pp. 10–11.

4 The National Advisory Council on the Training and Supply of Teachers (NACTST) was established in June 1949, "to keep under review national policy on the training and conditions of qualification of teachers, and on the recruitment and distribution of teachers in ways best calculated to meet the needs of the schools or other educational establishments". See *Education in 1949*, pp. 45–46.

CHAPTER TWENTY-TWO

Three-year Course

From 1946 to 1954 the increasing number of teachers barely kept pace with the increasing number of children in the schools. Then the ratio improved, thanks to "buoyant recruitment, later retirement, and the continued willingness of married women to remain in or return to teaching".[1] The trend persisted in 1955. At last, thought many people, it will be possible to lengthen the two-year college course to three years.

The NACTST had, in fact, anticipated this possibility some years previously. One of its first acts had been to appoint a sub-committee to consider whether it would be practicable to introduce the three-year course, and if so, when? The sub-committee had reported in 1952 that in its opinion introduction could not be before 1960, because the schools would absorb all the teachers that could be trained in the 1950s.

The 1954 figures, however, prompted the Association of Teachers in Colleges and Departments of Education (ATCDE)[2] to urge the Minister of Education, Sir David (later Lord) Eccles, to fix a date for the introduction of the three-year course. He referred the matter to the NACTST, asking it to advise him about:

1 The educational advantages of a three-year course.

2 What form it should take.

3 By what method it should be introduced.

4 The factors that must be considered in deciding a date.

The NACTST reported early in 1956, and the Minister published the report in September. In brief, it said:

1 Prospective teachers needed three years' training if they were to be the mature, well-educated, and highly skilled teachers demanded by the 1944 Education Act.

2 The three years should form a continuous period of training planned as a whole.

3 The three-year course should be introduced everywhere simultaneously.

4 The early years of the 1960s would offer a particularly favourable, and possibly unique, opportunity for its introduction.

The NACTST thought "the choice lay between 1959 and 1960".[3] It urged the Minister to fix the date as soon as possible, because the colleges would need at least two years to make preparations. Just over twelve months later, on 6 June 1957, the Government announced that it had decided upon September 1960. Most people welcomed the news, but a minority, especially among those who gave absolute priority to reducing the size of classes, thought 1960 too early.

It is one of the larger ironies of English educational history that the reason for effecting this reform—which had been desired by teachers, administrators, and HMI, for many years—was, of all things, fear of unemployment among teachers. The NACTST said so explicitly.

> Without introduction of the three-year course or some other equivalent restriction of recruitment (and without some major new source of demand for teachers), it is not impossible that there may be some difficulty in the early 1960s ... in maintaining full employment in the teaching profession.[4]

"In such circumstances," continued the NACTST, "it seems wise not to bank up too many teachers so soon, but rather to adjust the flow of training in good time by the introduction of the three-year course." The report made it crystal clear that by adjustment of the flow of training the NACTST meant a permanent large reduction in the number of teachers produced by the colleges.

> There is no case for expanding the number of training places available to enable the three-year course to be introduced without reducing the output of trained teachers ... introduction must mean a reduction by about one-third in the output from the present two-year colleges.[5]

The NACTST case was apparently based on two alarming assumptions: (1) neither the raising of the school leaving age nor the introduction of compulsory part-time continued education was contemplated for the near future; (2) there was no need to improve the existing pupil-teacher ratios. Happily, the schools were saved from the consequences of such lamentably misconceived advice by forces beyond the control of the NACTST. The birth-rate began to rise again, more pupils stayed at school beyond the leaving age than had been expected, and increasing numbers of women teachers left the profession in order to get married or start a family. The NACTST had reached its conclusions on the basis of projections showing that the net annual increase in the number of teachers in maintained schools (if the two-year course continued) would be about 7,000 up to 1961, and 6,000 thereafter. But the 1957 figures gave a net increase of only 4,400—under two-thirds of what had been predicted.

To the Government's credit, it did not go back on its decision to introduce the three-year course in 1960. It announced in June 1958 an interim building programme designed to provide 2,500 additional training college places as quickly as possible. In July it was advised by the NACTST that altogether about 16,000 places would be needed; to increase the total accommodation in the training colleges (exclusive of the specialist colleges) to 36,000, and thus give an annual output from a three-year course of 12,000 teachers. That, said the NACTST, should give a net annual increase in the teaching force of 6,000, which should be sufficient to eliminate over-large classes by 1968—another projection that was to prove sadly mistaken.

In September the Minister of Education, Mr Geoffrey Lloyd, announced that, while not prepared to commit himself to 16,000 places, he was authorising 12,000, including the 2,500 of the interim programme, to be completed by September 1962. Almost everyone told him that 12,000 was not enough; and they were right. In June 1959 another 4,000 were added, and even this was soon to be judged insufficient. Early in 1960 Sir David Eccles, now Minister for the second time, ordered another 8,000, and speeded up the time schedule to finish the entire programme by September 1966. Thus within two years—1958 to 1960—a total of 24,000 additional places was authorised. This would double the capacity of the general training colleges.

"So big an expansion offered a unique chance of re-shaping the training college system," wrote the Minister in 1961.[6] The opportunity was, in fact, a two-fold one: to re-shape both the physical structure and the content of the training. By 1960 there were obvious changes in the structure. Many colleges had become much larger (and consequently ideas about the optimum size for a college were changing dramatically). The number of mixed colleges had almost trebled: from 16 to 44. A day training college for mature students, who were being recruited in increasing numbers, had been opened in Leeds (the James Graham College), and several more were on the stocks.

Change in the content of training was also on the way. Systematic discussion of a three-year course had begun, in training colleges, Institutes and Schools of Education, and teachers' organisations, as early as 1955, two full years before the Government announced the date of its introduction. Exploratory talks revealed general agreement on two principles: (1) the longer period should be used not so much to introduce more matter as to enable students to work in less hurried fashion, and (2) the number of formal classes and lectures should be reduced, and the time thus saved given to seminars, tutorials, and private study. (Some radical reformers wanted to add "and to unscheduled pursuits selected by the student".)

It was agreed that the two major elements in the two-year course should be retained: study of the theory and practice of education, and, primarily for personal enrichment, study of one or two subjects ordinarily included in school curricula; and that, as previously, the two should proceed concurrently. Most people wished to add a compulsory course in English, biased towards its use as a means of communication. Many wanted a survey of contemporary affairs, many an introduction to the sociological background of education. A strong body of opinion desired compulsory mathematics, and compulsory science had its advocates.

About two crucial issues, both of which had been battle-grounds of controversy since training began, there was no agreement: (1) whether the main emphasis in the course should be on personal education or professional training, and (2) whether in the professional training the emphasis should be on theory or practice. From the autumn of 1957 thinking about these issues was considerably influenced by a Ministry of Education booklet which offered suggestions for a three-year course.[7] Its authors, HMIs experienced in training college work, considered that "the most substantial changes following from the extension of the course ... should be in the academic work", because:

> It is important for the health of the teaching profession as a whole that three-year training should give a considerable proportion of teachers an academic standing and confidence which will enable them to take their places alongside graduates.[8]

They rejected the view—which they acknowledged was widely held—that much of the additional time should be given to Education. Professional studies, they thought, might "benefit more from a re-arrangement of the course", and from the greater maturity of third-year students, than from the allocation of more time.

As time went on, staff discussions tended to concentrate more and more on two points: (1) the optimum length and incidence of teaching practice, and (2) the standard of attainment in academic studies to be expected by the end of the third year. About the total amount of time to be given to school practice there was no great dispute; it was generally agreed that it should be proportionately not more than was given in the two-year course, and possibly rather less: that is, not more than 90 days, but not fewer than 60. This agreement was not, however, so united as might at first sight appear, because there were at least two opinions about what should be included in 'School Practice'. Did this include visits to schools by students for purposes of observation, or the teaching of small groups of children by students under the direction of a class teacher? The college staffs in the Sheffield Institute area said "No" to both these questions, insisting that 'School Practice' meant teaching a whole class. They were, however, prepared to be satisfied with 60 days of this, thus leaving a margin for observation and other forms of experience in schools.

Many Institutes seem to have left the terms 'School Practice' and 'Teaching Practice' undefined. Hull, exceptionally, thought that:

> all students do not require the same period of practice ... a minimum of twelve weeks and a maximum of eighteen weeks should be allowed with discretionary powers left to the training colleges to allot the time appropriate for the individual student.[9]

Other opinions about teaching practice were more conventional, but they were widely various. There were devotees of practice early in the course, and of deferral to the latter part; of long practices and short practices; of block practice versus one-day or one half-day a week, and vice versa. They all ground their axes industriously, but no consensus was achieved.

The debate about standards of attainment in Main subjects was similarly inconclusive. The HMIs' booklet suggested that at the end of a three-year course there would be a greater difference between abler and less able students than in a two-year course. To meet this, the authors proposed that Main courses should be available at two levels: A and B. For A, a standard comparable with that of a pass degree would be required, for B, that of the Teacher's Certificate. In principle, this idea (which was not new), was generally accepted, but its implementation raised a crop of questions. If students taking A level courses had to reach degree standard, why not award them a degree? If students could take two Main subjects, could both be at A level, or should one be at A, the other at B? Could a student qualify for a Certificate on one B? If the range of options was from two As to one B, would it not make nonsense of the idea of a pass standard?

In some areas such problems were exacerbated by attempts to link Main with Curriculum courses. Bristol, for example, devised an elaborate scheme specifying how many Curriculum courses must be taken, respectively, by prospective Primary or Secondary school teachers. The function of Curriculum courses was disputed, often with some heat. This was not surprising, for such courses varied greatly in both depth and duration. At the one extreme were 'basic', or 'remedial', courses whose function was little more than to give students confidence, at the other courses involving rigorous study of methodology.

Opinions differed about how many Curriculum courses a student ought to take. Some wanted to free the prospective Secondary school teacher from doing any at all; others thought he should do at least one or two. For prospective Primary school teachers, the extremists demanded as many as five Curriculum subjects; the moderates protested, not without reason, that this would mean too heavy a load on a student. The debate inevitably raised the question of whether there should be any compulsory Curriculum courses at all. Opinions were, of course, divided.

Many cognate problems were also discussed, often at interminable length, during the years 1955 to 1959. Decisions had, however, to be taken by the summer of 1959, in order that applicants for the three-year course due to start in September 1960 could be told in the autumn (when applications would begin) what they were in for. The necessity led to some last-minute rushes.

Despite the widely repeated assertion that the introduction of the three-year course offered a unique opportunity to make fundamental changes in training college courses, the courses which emerged from the long debate were not in general very different from the two-year courses. The following are more or less typical.

SHEFFIELD

1 The course to consist of Education (theory and practice), Main subjects, Curriculum subjects, and English.

2 Not less than the equivalent of 120 half-days to be devoted to teaching in school as an active member of staff. Observation, and the teaching of small groups of children, to be additional.

3 Students to take one *or* two Main subjects, at one of two levels.

4 Students to take, in addition to Main subjects, Curriculum subjects.

5 All students not exempted by the Principal of the College, and not taking English as a Main subject, to do a course in English lasting throughout the first two years. At the Principal's discretion, this course could be extended into the third year for weak students.

6 Attainment in Education and Main subjects to be examined by the University at the end of the three years. Attainment in Curriculum subjects and English to be assessed by the College and certified by the Principal.

BRISTOL

1 All students to take throughout the course a study of the theory and practice of education.

2 All students to undertake:

(i) study of *either* one *or* two Special subjects, *or* of one Special subject and a Second subject;

(ii) a general course in English for at least two years; and

(iii) courses in such other subjects as the college determined.

3 A Special subject to be studied as a Main subject throughout the course, a Second subject to be studied as a Main subject for two years only. Other subjects to be studied for not less than one year.

4 Students to satisfy the examiners in theory and practice of education, Special and Second subjects, and the general course in English, and to give evidence of a satisfactory level of professional competence in other subjects.

Bristol decided to test students by continuous assessment, the method its UDE had used since 1919.

WALES

1 All students to undertake a course in the Principles of Education and practical teaching.

2 All students to be required to take at least one Main course, at one of two levels. No student to be permitted to take more than one Main course at the advanced level, but a second Main course might be taken at ordinary level.

3 Where necessary, students to take other courses according to their needs.

4 Every student's course to include English (and Welsh where appropriate), mathematics, and health education, including physical education.

5 Students to be examined, at the end of the third year, by the University in Principles and Practice of Education, and Main subjects. All other parts of the course to be assessed by the college.

Over the country there was a wide range of decisions about Main courses. Birmingham insisted on students taking *either* two Principal subjects *or* one Principal and one other subject. Leeds required one advanced level Main subject supported by two or more subjects studied with relevance to school work. Sheffield allowed anything from two Main subjects at A level to one at B. Durham asked simply for one or more Main subjects. London restricted students to one Main subject.

Such diversity in the programmes of the Institutes and Schools of Education was typical of the English tradition of individual freedom and initiative. This tradition has its weaknesses as well as its strengths; it concedes, for example, the liberty to experiment—or not to experiment. During the 1960s not so much experimenting was done by the colleges as could have been desired, doubtless because of the problems presented by expansion. On the other hand, most people felt that the general improvement in the standard of work was better than they had expected.

References

1 *Education in 1955*, p. 10.
2 The ATCDE was formed in 1943 by the amalgamation of the lecturers' and principals' associations. On 1 January 1976 it merged with the Association of Teachers in Technical Institutions (ATTI) to form the National Association of Teachers in Further and Higher Education (NATFHE).
3 *Three Year Training for Teachers*. Fifth Report of the National Advisory Council on the Training and Supply of Teachers. HMSO, 1956, p. 44.
4 ibid., p. 11.
5 ibid., p. 7.
6 *Education in 1960*, p. 69.
7 *The Training of Teachers*: Suggestions for a three year training college course. Ministry of Education Pamphlet No. 34. HMSO, 1957.
8 ibid., pp. 2 and 3.
9 Private communication to the author.

CHAPTER TWENTY-THREE

Towards a Graduate Profession

Five months after the three-year course began, the Prime Minister, Mr Harold Macmillan, appointed a committee, with as chairman Professor Lord Robbins, "to review the pattern of full-time higher education in Great Britain and ... advise Her Majesty's Government on what principles its long-term development should be based". The committee was asked especially for advice on:

> whether there should be any changes in that pattern, whether any new types of institution are desirable and whether any modifications should be made in the present arrangements for planning and co-ordinating the development of the various types of institutions.[1]

The Report of the 'Robbins' Committee was published in October 1963. It gave considerable attention to the education and training of school teachers. It noted that:

> The Training Colleges in England and Wales and Colleges of Education in Scotland alike feel themselves to be only doubtfully recognised as part of the system of higher education and yet to have attained standards of work and a characteristic ethos that justify their claim to an appropriate place in it.[2]

The remedy for this, thought the Committee, was for the colleges to "go forward in closer association with the universities not only on the academic but also on the administrative side".[3] To this end it advocated a return to the McNair Committee's concept of association, and recommended that:

The colleges in each university's Institute of Education and the University Department of Education should be formed into a School of Education.[4]

The Committee added three further recommendations, calculated to raise the status of the colleges: (1) they should have independent governing bodies; (2) they should be financed by ear-marked grants, made through their universities; and (3) they should provide, not only three-year courses leading to the Teacher's Certificate, but also four-year courses leading to a degree as well as the Certificate. This 'Bachelor of Education' (BEd) degree would be awarded by the university with which a college was associated.

The Government welcomed closer academic ties between universities and training colleges—henceforth to be called 'Colleges of Education'—but turned down the idea of administrative and financial integration. It also refused to consider independent governing bodies for the colleges, but softened this blow by inviting them to join a study group on their internal government. It agreed to a four-year course and the award of a BEd degree.

Discussions between universities and colleges about this degree began immediately. There were many snags. Some universities were at first reluctant to undertake the responsibility of validating such a degree. Several shrank from including it in the 'practical' subjects—art and crafts, domestic science, music, physical education—largely though these loomed in college curricula. There were disputes about entry qualifications, about when, and how, students should be selected for the fourth year, and about where most of the teaching for the degree should be done, and by whom.

The most serious trouble was caused by the refusal of over half the universities concerned to offer more than General or Pass degrees. In 1968, when all the twenty-one universities with Institutes (or Schools) of Education had agreed to award BEd degrees, only seven were prepared to offer classified honours degrees.[5] Three others would give an unclassified honours degree, and would guarantee this to be of good standard.[6] But eleven would give only 'General', 'Ordinary', or 'Pass' degrees.[7]

The first BEd degrees were awarded in 1968, by the Universities of Keele, Leeds, Reading, Sheffield, and Sussex. In 1969 all the twenty-one universities made awards. But for some years thereafter the number of candidates for a fourth year, and consequently the number of graduates, remained small; not until 1972 did it reach ten per cent of the number of third year students. (It had always been agreed that only 'suitable students' should be accepted for a fourth year, but ten per cent was a far call from the 25 per cent for whom the Robbins Committee had assumed provision should be made by the mid-1970s.)[8]

The small numbers were due partly to the relatively high entry qualifications imposed by both universities and colleges, but more to the fact that a considerable proportion—estimated in 1972 at over one-quarter— of the students who qualified for a fourth year did not take up the option. The proportion was, not surprisingly, highest in those areas where selection of students was deferred until the Teacher's Certificate results were known, that is, after the end of the third year. Faced with an agonising choice of taking a job or waiting in hope, many students opted for safety.

The anomalies in the BEd structure—the different entry qualifications, different dates at which selection was made, different types of degree awarded—were severely criticised by a Select Committee of the House of Commons which investigated teacher education and training during the Parliamentary session of 1969–70. The lack of consultation and co-ordination, said the chairman of the Committee, Mr F T Willey, MP, in a book published in 1971, had resulted in "such confusion as to seriously damage the standing of the degree, and the risk of permanently debasing its value".[9]

In 1969 the BEd was made available to serving teachers with five or more years of experience.[10] The first course, which was heavily over-subscribed, was started in January 1970 by Lancaster University. It comprised a preparatory year of part-time directed study followed by a year full-time at one of the University's associated colleges of education.

In 1972 the Council for National Academic Awards (CNAA) also began validating BEd degrees. The possibility of its doing so had been suggested as early as 1966, when the Secretary of State, Mr Anthony Crosland, invited five LEAs[11] to set up, as an experiment, teacher training departments in major technical colleges. The selected colleges, however, all decided to join Institutes of Education and accept university validation. It was not until six years later that one of them, by then incorporated in the Sunderland Polytechnic, turned to the CNAA. The first course was a three-year part-time one for serving teachers which included one residential week-end each term and an annual summer school of a fortnight's duration. It consisted entirely of professional studies.

In June 1973 the University Grants Committee (UGC) and the CNAA jointly appointed a Study Group "to draw up guidelines for a new Bachelor of Education degree". The Group's report, published in May 1974, said that the degree proposed would differ from existing BEds in that:

> it will be designed ... as a course of higher education in which the initial training of a teacher is integrated, rather than being based on qualification through the Certificate in Education course.[12]

The degree, for which candidates would be accepted on the same basis as for other undergraduate courses, would be validated by both universities and the CNAA.

In 1972 the Open University (OU) began to take a hand. From September of that year students at the Milton Keynes College of Education (whose buildings were adjacent to the OU headquarters), could if they wished take an OU BA course instead of the Oxford University BEd. If they chose the OU course they could either (1) spend three years in college, acquiring there five of the six 'Credits' required for a pass degree, and getting the sixth by part-time study while teaching, or (2) spend four years in college securing the eight Credits needed for an honours degree.

The content of a BEd course varied in the early days as widely, and illogically, as any other feature of the degree. For the Liverpool University general degree, for example, study of the principles and practice of education had to be accompanied by study of two other subjects, one of which must be studied throughout the four years. For the honours degree at Sussex University only one other subject was required, but there was a 'linking study' designed to show the relationship between that subject and the principles and practice of education.

Not least varied were the part-time courses. As has been noted, the first one at Sunderland Polytechnic consisted entirely of professional studies: the philosophy, psychology, and sociology of education, curriculum theory, and study of a particular age-group of children.

The course started in September 1974 at the Polytechnic of North London (PNL) for Secondary school and Further Education teachers comprised educational theory, one other subject, and a linking study whose function was to keep the course directly relevant to classroom work, to which end it included investigations in schools made by students. This course was unusual in offering an honours degree after three years.

Other important innovations made during the 1960s included the experimental use of closed circuit television (CCTV) as a teaching aid in colleges of education, and the reforms in the colleges' internal government brought about as the result of the recommendations made by the study group chaired by Mr T R (later Sir Toby) Weaver.

In the opening years of the 1960s one or two training colleges began tentatively to experiment with CCTV. In 1964 the Secretary of State, Mr Anthony Crosland, invited eleven colleges to explore its possibilities, especially as a means for enabling students to observe school children at work. The colleges were selected to form two groups, one in the north of England and the other in the south, and their researches were collated respectively by the University Institutes of Education at Leeds and London. In 1966, following the first report from the Institutes, the Secretary of State asked that the experiment be extended, especially to cover videotape recording. The response to his request was so large that in 1967 he had regretfully to tell the colleges to restrict their provision; his Department had not enough money to allow them all to cover the entire CCTV range.

The report of the study group on *The Government of Colleges of Education,* which was published in March 1966, recommended that the governing bodies of maintained colleges, which currently had to be sub-committees of the Education Committee, should be made independent bodies representative of the LEA, the associated university, the academic staff, local teachers, and "persons with a concern for teacher training or specialist subjects". A governing body would delegate to the academic board of a college the power to deal with all academic matters. The necessary legislative sanction needed for some of the proposed reforms was embodied in the Education (No. 2) Act 1968, which also dealt with the government of Further Education colleges and Special schools.

In the last month of this decade the Secretary of State, Mr Edward (later Lord) Short, ended an anomaly that had long been a source of grievance to many teachers by requiring that for service in maintained schools graduates must be trained. The order did not affect those already in service. For Primary schools it applied to all graduating after 31 December 1969, for Secondary schools from December 1973.[13]

References

1 *Higher Education*: Report of the Committee appointed by the Prime Minister under the chairmanship of Lord Robbins 1961–63, HMSO 1963, p. iii.
2 ibid., p. 107.
3 ibid., p. 119.
4 ibid., p. 279.
5 Bristol, Lancaster, Leeds, Leicester, London, Reading, Sussex.
6 Keele, Southampton, Warwick.
7 Birmingham, Durham, Exeter, Hull, Liverpool, Manchester, Newcastle, Nottingham, Oxford, Sheffield, Wales.
8 *Higher Education*, p. 116.
9 Willey, F T, and Maddison, R E, *An Enquiry into Teacher Training*, University of London Press, 1971, p. 67.
10 See Circulars 10/69 and 19/69, dated respectively 20 May 1969 and 16 December 1969. The May Circular set out an interim scheme.
11 Barking, Inner London Education Authority (ILEA), Manchester, Nottingham, Sunderland.
12 Quoted from *The Times Higher Education Supplement*, 17 May 1974, p. 18.
13 See Circular 18/69, "Professional Training for Teachers in Maintained Schools", dated 10 December 1969.

CHAPTER TWENTY-FOUR

End of an Era

During the later 1960s there arose a widespread demand for a thorough investigation of the education and training of teachers in England and Wales. Hostile critics alleged that the entire system was out-of-date, that the ATOs were ineffective, the government of the colleges authoritarian, the teaching poor, the curriculum irrelevant to the work of the schools, and the standard of the Teacher's Certificate low. Defenders of the colleges also desired an inquiry, on the grounds that it would refute these charges, dispel public ignorance of the work of the colleges, and reveal the striking advances they were making.

For some years the DES resisted the demand, arguing that while the colleges were expanding rapidly they should not be loaded with extraneous burdens. Not until February 1970 did it give way, and then only to the extent that the Secretary of State, Mr Edward Short, asked the ATOs to examine their current practices, and suggest ways of improving them.

During the previous autumn, however, a Select Committee of the House of Commons which had been appointed in 1968 to investigate the entire spectrum of Education and Science had turned its attention to the training of teachers. In the Parliamentary session of 1969–70 it took a great deal of evidence about this from many organisations and individuals. The general election of October 1970 put an end to the Committee, but the evidence it had accumulated was published by HM Stationery Office, and its chairman, Mr F T Willey, MP, with a colleague published a book summarising the criticisms made of the system.[1]

In December 1970 the Secretary of State, Now Mrs Margaret Thatcher, appointed a Committee of Inquiry, under the chairmanship of Lord James of Rusholme, Vice-Chancellor of York University, with the following terms of reference:

> In the light of the review currently being undertaken by the Area Training Organisations, and of the evidence published by the Select Committee on Education and Science, to enquire into the present arrangements for the education, training and probation of teachers in England and Wales and in particular to examine:
>
> (i)   what should be the content and organisation of courses to be provided;
>
> (ii) whether a larger proportion of intending teachers should be educated with students who have not chosen their careers or chosen other careers;
>
> (iii) what, in the context of (i) and (ii) above, should be the role of the maintained and voluntary colleges of education, the polytechnics and other further education institutions maintained by local education authorities, and the universities
>
> and to make recommendations.

The committee was asked to work full-time, and to report, if possible, within twelve months.

The 'James' Report was published in February 1972.[2] It offered a novel and ingenious, but extremely controversial, scheme of education and training consisting of three 'Cycles': (1) personal education, (2) pre-service training and induction, (3) in-service education and training.

In Cycle 1, prospective teachers intending to teach one or two subjects to a relatively high level would, as previously, take a degree course lasting ordinarily three years. All others would take a two-year course leading to a proposed new qualification, a Diploma in Higher Education (Dip HE). This course would not be restricted to prospective teachers, but open to all candidates with the required entry qualifications.

Cycle 2 would last two years. Students would spend the first year in a college or department of education, doing studies concentrated upon "preparation for work appropriate to a teacher at the beginning of his career rather than on formal courses in 'educational theory' ".[3]

The second year would be spent in a school. During this year students would have the status of 'licensed teacher', which meant that they would be salaried members of staff, but under supervision. They would not teach full-time; one-fifth of their working week would be spent under instruction at a 'professional centre'.

Cycle 3, to which the Committee gave "the highest priority", would comprehend "the whole range of activities by which teachers can extend their personal education, develop their professional competence and improve their understanding of educational principles and techniques".[4] It would last throughout their teaching careers, and would include entitlement to "release with pay for a minimum of one school term ... in a specified number of years"—every seven years to begin with, and later every five.[5]

Reactions to the Report were extremely varied; but in general Cycle 3 was warmly welcomed, Cycle 2 almost universally rejected, and Cycle 1 given a mixed reception that ranged from cordial approbation to apprehensive dislike.

The Government's reaction came eleven months later, in a White Paper, *Education: A Framework for Expansion,* published in December 1972. This comprehended almost every branch of public education, but gave most of its attention to higher education, including the education and training of teachers.

It said that the Government accepted the six objectives at which the James Committee had aimed:

1 a large and systematic expansion of in-service training;

2 a planned reinforcement of the process of induction;

3 the progressive achievement of an all-graduate profession;

4 the improvement of the training of teachers in Further Education;

5 the whole-hearted acceptance of the colleges of education into the family of higher education institutions;

6 improved arrangements for the control and co-ordination of teacher training and supply, both nationally and regionally.[6]

While the Government accepted Cycle 3, it rejected Cycle 2, holding (as did almost all professional opinion) that it allowed insufficient time for teaching practice. It accepted Cycle 1, and the DipHE with the proviso that this award "must be made generally acceptable as a terminal qualification" which gave entry into employment, and as "a foundation for further study" which would earn credits towards other qualifications, including degrees. To allow this, "the normal minimum entry qualifications [for DipHE courses] should be the same as for degrees", and the courses "no less demanding intellectually than the first two years of a course at degree level".[7]

The most crucial sentences about the colleges of education in the White Paper were those concerning their future.

> Some colleges either singly or jointly should develop ... into major institutions of higher education concentrating on the arts and human sciences, with particular reference to their application in teaching and other professions.[8]

Suggestions not altogether dissimilar from these had been made by the Robbins Committee.

> Some colleges will wish to broaden their scope by providing courses, with a measure of common studies, for entrants to various professions in the social services ... Other colleges may wish to provide general courses in arts or science subjects.[9]

But Robbins had rejected any idea of detaching the training colleges from the universities; on the contrary, it wanted the links between them to be strengthened. It had even suggested that:

> It may be appropriate for some colleges, perhaps particularly those that broaden their scope beyond the training of teachers, to become individually constituent parts of a university. Others might combine with a leading technical college to form a new university or to become part of one.[10]

The James Committee similarly took it for granted that the universities and the colleges of education would continue to work together. Although it felt that the time had come for "major modifications" of the existing relationship between them, "it would be folly," it asserted, "to dissociate the universities from teacher education and training."[11] It skirted cautiously round the question of amalgamations, not ruling them out, but apparently thinking of them mainly as mergers of two or more colleges of education. "Larger questions would arise," it thought, "if it were decided that a few colleges should change their status and function altogether by amalgamation with universities or polytechnics."[12]

The White Paper tackled those "larger questions". It judged the colleges of education—or some of them—to be "admirably" equipped "to share in the expansion of higher education". But not within the university sector. On this point the Government differed radically from both Robbins and James. It did not exclude the possibility of colleges of education amalgamating with universities, but it laid down conditions which made such amalgamations improbable.

> To be fully effective educationally such integration would need ... to be complete ... staff, students and courses would need to become equal and integral parts of the institution concerned.[13]

The Government's mind was clearly concentrated on the idea of "major institutions of higher education" in the public sector, not the university. In addition to those colleges of education it believed capable, "either singly or jointly", of achieving that status, others would be "encouraged to combine forces with neighbouring polytechnics or other colleges of further education to fill a somewhat similar role".[14]

But there was an awkward snag; many of the 160 or so colleges of education were "comparatively small and inconveniently located for development into larger general purpose institutions". For these a variety of futures was predicted.

> Some ... will continue to be needed exclusively for purposes of teacher education with increasing emphasis on in-service rather than initial training. Some may seek greater strength by reciprocal arrangements with the Open University on the lines of the experiment recently initiated.[15] Others may find a place in the expansion of teachers' and professional centres. Some must face the possibility that in due course they will have to be converted to new purposes; some may need to close.[16]

Reactions in the colleges ranged from heady exhilaration at the thought of becoming one of the "major institutions of higher education" to cold fear of being closed. Many of the larger colleges—too many, as it proved—proclaimed their intention of 'going it alone', foreseeing for themselves a glamorous future as they grew in size and status. Some were soon disillusioned, but in the event more started on a new career as 'free-standing colleges' than apparently the Government had anticipated. (How many will survive in that status only the future can tell.)

In many medium-sized colleges there was widespread apprehension that "to combine forces" with a polytechnic or college of further education was a euphemism for "be swallowed up by". Among the smaller colleges some began to cast round anxiously for allies in an expected struggle to resist closure.

Apprehension was intensified by the DES Circular 7/73, *Development of Higher Education in the non-University sector,* issued in May 1973. This made clear beyond any doubt that the Government intended most colleges of education to find their future in the public sector of a precisely delimited binary system of higher education; and that this was to happen in the near future. The Circular asked the LEAs to submit by November 'interim' proposals for their maintained colleges. Final plans would have to be deferred until the new local authorities being set up under the Local Government Act 1972 took over on 1 April 1974, but the DES requested that these be submitted as soon as possible after that date.

What was wanted, the LEAs were told—and this was the nub of the matter—was "not merely the planning of a marginal expansion of higher education ... but rather a major reconsideration of the future role of colleges of education both in and outside teacher training".[17]

Most of the LEAs made their interim submissions by, or shortly after, the deadline of 30 November 1973. There followed protracted discussions: between LEAs and their colleges, LEAs and the DES, voluntary colleges and the DES, and voluntary colleges and LEAs. Most were amicable if at moments tense, but there were some where opposing views clashed fiercely, as at Brighton, where the college of education and the university wished to merge, but the LEA desired the college to amalgamate with the polytechnic. A similar conflict occurred later at Coventry. Some of the bitterest battles were fought over proposed closures, especially where, as for example in the new county of Hereford and Worcester, the question was which of two colleges should be closed. Needless to say, Culham once again figured among those sentenced to death.

In August 1975 the DES announced that the futures of over 1.10.

colleges in England had been decided. (Information about those in Wales was to follow later.) A dozen colleges were to "discontinue initial training". Of the others, it seemed that about one-quarter would be 'free-standing', that is, single institutions providing teacher training and other courses, one-quarter would merge with poly- technics, one-quarter with further education colleges, and one-quarter with other colleges of education.

But these were far from being the final figures. As the birthrate continued to decline the DES repeatedly revised downwards its estimate of the school population in the coming years, and consequently of the number of teacher training places that would be required. At the time when this book went to press (March 1977) the figure for the latter had fallen to 45,000—and at least 25 more colleges were threatened with closure.

On 1 August 1975 new regulations for further education[18] became operative which officially ended the 'McNair' era of teacher training. Reflecting the Government's policy that "outside the universities, teacher education and further education should be assimilated into a common system",[19] they ended "the overall supervision of teacher training through Area Training Organisations, including advice to the Secretary of State on the approval of persons as teachers in schools",[20] and the provisions (previously laid down in regulations for the training of teachers) governing "the duration, standards, and academic supervision of courses of initial training, and the eligibility of students for admission to training".[21]

On 1 January 1976 the Association of Teachers in Colleges and Departments of Education (ATCDE) amalgamated with the Associ- ation of Teachers in Technical Institutions (ATTI) to constitute the National Association of Teachers in Further and Higher Education (NATFHE). In February a new Burnham Committee for Further Education was formed by merging the Pelham Committee, the Farm Institutes Committee, and the old Burnham FE Committee. These had previously negotiated separately the salaries of teachers in colleges of education, farm institutes, and FE colleges.

Thus has ended a system of teacher education and training which had endured for nearly two centuries. Throughout that long period the training college curriculum, and the methods employed to apply it, though progressively altered and improved in detail, remained basically the same. The system had many defects, but it was not without its virtues. It has been deliberately destroyed. One can only hope that its successor, whatever form this may ultimately take, will be sufficiently better to justify its execution.

References

1 Willey, F T, and Maddison, R E, opt. cit.
2 *Teacher Education and Training*: A Report by a Committee of Inquiry appointed by the Secretary of State for Education and Science, under the chairmanship of Lord James of Rusholme. HMSO, 1972.
3 ibid., p. 23.
4 ibid., p. 5.
5 ibid., p. 12.
6 *Education: A Framework for Expansion.* HMSO, 1972, p. 16.
7 ibid., pp. 32–33.
8 ibid., p. 44.
9 *Higher Education*, p. 108.
10 ibid.
11 *Teacher Education and Training*, p. 49.
12 ibid., p. 62.
13 *Education: A Framework for Expansion*, p. 44.
14 ibid.
15 At Milton Keynes. See Chapter 23.
16 *Education: A Framework for Expansion*, p. 44.
17 Circular 7/73, para. 4.
18 *The Further Education Regulations 1975* (SI 1975/1054).
19 ibid., p. 1, para. 2.
20 ibid., para. 3(a).
21 ibid., p. 3, para. 6, (b) and (c).

For further reading and reference

Only a few of the many sources of information are given here; for a much larger list see *Teacher Training Institutions in England and Wales*: A bibliographical guide to their history, by Michael Berry, Society for Research into Higher Education Ltd, 25 Northampton Square, London EC1, 1973.

For the nineteenth century the annual reports of the Committee of Council on Education are invaluable; each contains detailed reports by HMI on their districts and on individual colleges. Publication of such reports was unfortunately discontinued when the Board of Education took over in 1900. The annual reports of the Board and its successors include chapters on teacher training. Among other official reports those of the Cross Commission (1888), the Departmental Committee on the Pupil-Teacher System (1898), the Departmental Committee on the Training of Teachers for Public Elementary Schools (1925), and the McNair Report are essential.

Sir James Kay-Shuttleworth's *Four Periods of Public Education: As reviewed in 1832, 1839, 1846, 1862*, is a mine of information. R W Rich's *The Training of Teachers in England and Wales during the 19th century* is a well-documented survey. G E Lance Jones's *Training of Teachers in England and Wales* (Oxford University Press, 1924) describes the system in the early 1920s. For the late 1940s see C A Richardson in *The Education of Teachers in England, France and USA* (Unesco, 1953). *The University Connection*, by W R Niblett, D W Humphreys, and J R Fairhurst (NFER, 1975), describes in detail the periods of the Joint Examining Boards and the ATOs.

Histories of individual colleges and departments of education are regrettably few. Those about Darlington, Dartford, Derby, Goldsmiths', Hull Municipal college, St Hild's, Durham, Sheffield, and Westminster are mentioned in the text. Others include Chester, by John L Bradbury, Lincoln, by D H J Zebedee, F L Calder, by Margaret Scott, Culham, by Leonard Naylor, Didsbury, by A H Body and N J Frangopulo, and the Newcastle UDE, by J C Tyson and J P Tuck.

Among periodicals *The Schoolmaster* (from 1870), *Education* (from 1903), and *The Times Educational Supplement* (from 1910) give much news and comment. From 1971 *The Times Higher Education Supplement* is most helpful.

Index

ST. PATRICK'S
COLLEGE

LIBRARY